CW01663465

This book is dedicated to my wonderful dad x

# Table Of Contents:

## Part Two…

## Part Three…

# Part One:

# Chapter 1: Day One...

I was on my way back home from dropping the kids off to school, when I stopped in my tracks. There was a black slug on the ground. Black as night. I thought that was strange as we usually see slugs in a clear mucus colour closely followed by a smear of slim. This slug looked like something had taken everything that made him recognizable, and snatched it away. A flash back of my dad from last year eroded my mind. I looked closer, screwed my eyes half closed and asked myself...
"Do slugs get cancer?" What a thought to think. How had my mind brought it to this? But since April 2016...everything and anything could get the big 'C'. That was the month my dad was diagnosed with it...and my life changed forever. That was my 34th year in this world and I thought I knew everything. I thought I was prepared for anything, but it's funny how life changes you and prepares you for certain things...and doesn't for others.
I remember when I first moved over to England from America, (I'm an American Teabag as I like to think of myself...since I am an American and living in England. I'm also as small as a teabag with being only 5 ft 1) I was in my early twenties and going out most weekends to pubs or clubs. Out till one or two in the morning, and without a blink of an eye I would just walk home, on my own, from town to east Worthing, usually a 15/20 minute walk, with no worries about what could happen to me at all. My dad would have gone crazy at me if he had known. He would have shook his head with a tut, and say "Angie you need to look after yourself" Thankfully, at the time, he was living in America, and the most he would know about my life was whatever I wanted to share with him.I got married

to a handsome, responsible (for the most part, unless with his 4 other brothers of course) caring man, a couple of years after I moved to England. Matthew is such a loving husband. I just love the way he looks at me sometimes, it's as if he hasn't seen anything more beautiful than me, and I know I'm not anything amazing to look at…but sometimes he makes me feel like a goddess. We had two children and now because I know I am an important part of our family, I won't go out on my own past 6pm, unless in the summer and lighter outside. There's nothing like adding a bit of dark to make anything scary. I'm sure having children really opens your eyes to danger. It puts a whole new perspective on life. It highlights fears and shows you what is important to you.

Back in the day, before I got married, the most important thing to me was that I got to go out with my friends, have a good night and have plenty of time dancing before my feet couldn't cope, because I truly loved to dance. It didn't matter how much I was damaging my feet dancing for hours in heels, and it didn't matter that I really lacked sleep or how I was going to get home…dancing was what I loved.

Now all I can think about is, 'nothing can ever happen to me', because if anything did, who would look after my family, and that is constantly in my head. No more so than back in April when dad was diagnosed. It's mind boggling. I can completely see how people can have serious mental problems with this issue, because taken to great lengths, it could make you really unwell mentally. I guess anything that stems from love can be made right through love though. Talking about huge love…

I go to a wonderful church (ok, I can now hear you saying "not another religious book pushing more religion on to me" I am not pushing anything, i'm telling my story and my church just happened to be a part of it) anyway, I have been going to Elim church Worthing. This church has a brilliant pastor called Andrew. He has a fun way of teaching on a Sunday and one of my favourite things about him is his love for his family and friends. Most people know he will do anything for them. They will also know just how much he will do for a good pudding. This man definitely has a sweet tooth. I've been attending this church for the last 8 years, but i've really felt a special connection for the last year. This isn't to say I wasn't welcomed before, or that people didn't try to be my friend prior to this year, it's just I feel like I have true friends here now, that don't expect anything from me as well as I can really rely on from now onwards. I'm not saying you have to go to church to get these things, it's just I did. I'm part of a mid-week church group, and it is the most diverse, sweet, caring group I have ever been in.

There's Igor, the 'big Russian teddy bear' as I call him. He is such a soft, kind character but with that typical Russian accent. He is very knowledgeable but doesn't show off. There's Viv, married to big Russian teddy bear. She has the most amazing dimples. She enjoys expressing her thoughts but imagine someone who says what she thinks but doesn't want to upset anyone either, so she's always so apologetic . She is a very sweet lady with a big smile. Andrew is from Australia, as is his wife Lani. I call him the 'smiler'. No matter what he says, it always sounds joyful. He always just happens to be smiling, which makes me think he must have the best life. This brings me to his gorgeous wife Lani. Not only does she have beauty and brains but she is also the kindest person you will ever meet. She makes really excellent cakes…and I enjoy eating them for her. Maybe that's why our body shapes differ a bit.

There's Mark, who is probably the cool cat of the group. He can even play a saxophone. He's in his 40's but looks 12. He says to me that's because "black never cracks". He's got to be right because nobody looks that young after having 4 kids. He's married to a wonderful Irish nurse, Ruth, who also has found the secret to looking young. She doesn't go to our group because that is one of her night shift nights. She is the sweetest lady and it doesn't surprise me that she looks after people for her career. They both are wonderful godparents to my little boy and they are perfect for the job. We are so lucky.

Rita and Valentine are a sweet couple full of joy and happiness. Rita is a ray of sunshine with all the right things to say and Valentine is known as 'Dr Love'. Trish is a quiet sweet woman with a heart of gold. She takes shoe boxes to people in need in other countries over Christmas. And Carol, is another kind lady who would help anybody, she even has gone to Rwanda to help the children there.

Then there's Sally and Sam. Not a couple. Sally is married to Martin, but he goes to another group. She heads up the time for ladies team and makes sure all women know they are loved by the big man upstairs. Sam is another age defying male. He could run for the strongest man competitions with the head-sized muscles he has. He also has a brilliant smile that would make anyone feel happy. He works for a well known airline and is really good at his job. Another sweet lady is Yvonne. She has a soft voice and a big smile and shares my love of sweet things. She's married to BJ. He doesn't come at the moment because he is going through some loss in his own family. And last but not least, Corina and Alex. Corina is a sweet lady full of love and will do anything to help anyone. She is a beautiful lady inside and out. Alex is very relaxed laid back kind of guy with a very youthful face. He gives you tight loving hugs when he sees you like he really cares about you. A home group full of lots of wonderful genuine souls who continually support and encourage each other. This year I have really needed them and they have all been people I can lean on in this difficult time.

Matthew and I go every other Thursday evening while mum baby sits. It's mostly hosted by Mark but from time to time mark has to be in London or cant get home in time so then usually Sally will host at her house. Both houses I would just love to have. Mark's house is a fantastic family home with his massive kitchen-dining room and nice sized lounge oh and the toilet downstairs. And Sally's is amazing too with every room having an ensuite, and her massive garden. Either way, both very spacious and perfect in my eyes. So every other Thursday evening, Matthew and I put the kids to bed and then head over. We always bring some sort of nibbles, but nothing ever tastes quite as good as Lani's cakes. She is one of those types of ladies that can just whip up something amazing last minute, and quite often she miraculously finds a way of making it healthy as well. I remember once she actually made an amazing cake with tomatoes. Not a hint of tomato flavour to it either. The other thing about Lani's cakes is she never just brings a cake and puts it on the plate. She always puts such care into the presentation. If it's meant to have cream with it she'll bring a cute little jug with cream in it to pour on. If it's brownies she won't just bring them and hand them out in a plastic tub, she'll carefully arrange them on a long rectangle plate so it looks even more tempting.

The group meet from 8, although we always arrive early…I think because Matthew and I just can't wait to see everyone and it's suppose to finish at 9:30, but we always have a great discussion that always takes us over. I think Matthew and I would be there till Mark would have to kick us out, but we have to be home for mum because she always works the next day. It's hard leaving early but really we are so grateful for her helping us out. What would we do if she wasn't here? We don't have anyone else who could do it for us. We would just have to miss out. This would be such a shame as we have got so much out of this group. It's such a support network and a place where we can be ourselves and know that everyone likes us for who we are. Having family close is something I really treasure. Not just for the babysitting times, but for me, having family close is like having all your puzzle pieces fitting perfectly. It makes you smile within. Even when you argue with someone close, you still want them close to you because you still love them. For any daughters out there that are struggling to get on with your mums (we all do at some point)…this will pass. I struggled with our relationship from the early teenage years till really only recently since having kids. I think when you become a teenager it's very difficult because of all the hormones going wild in your body and having to cope with multiple things in life, on top of that your mum (or at least my mum) is always on you about tidying things up…that was literally my worst thing in the world. Funny thing is, now all I want is a tidy house and It's the hardest thing to have. This creates a lot of friction and sometimes your cup is so filled that you are ready to overspill…and usually mum is the person nearest, so even if you don't mean to stress on her, she is the one who gets it.

If I can offer any advice, it would be to try your hardest to do these 3 things before you do anything that could damage your relationship, family or health, and I only wish I had done this myself.

1. Breathe

2. Count to 10 before taking your next move

3. Think about; is it really worth it?

Whatever you are about to shout out. If after that you still feel it's important and it will help matters, go ahead. But if not, try and find a different way to let out your anger in a healthy way, because believe me, you will need her one day.

I talk to my mum everyday. It's usually a text in the morning to say "Hi" and "I'm tired, the kids woke up to early" and "How are you", but it's everyday and if either of us haven't text by 9am we feel like something is wrong. It's nice to have someone to share early mornings with and someone who no matter what will sympathise with you and be your cheerleader in whatever you choose to be doing. Yes sometimes we don't agree with each other, but we have learnt to tell each what is bothering us so we can move on.

# Chapter 2: That Day In April…

I don't remember what day of the week it was when I found out about my dad and  I don't remember what I had for dinner that night, but I completely remember the moment my dad's situation became serious. That moment when a prescription for antibiotics is just not going to fix anything. My brother, Paul, and I had been texting each other a lot more since my dad had started getting sick. Back then we thought it was something to do with his heart. Then one night, one of the kids woke me up and after I had dealt with them I checked my phone.

My brother had text saying he needed to talk to me, he couldn't handle it. This must have meant something quite serious because to me, Paul can cope with most things. He's the stronger one out of us both. So I went downstairs at 3:50am and told him to call me. This has always been a

problem for us. The 8 hour difference means that when i'm sleeping it's the best time to call him. We then had a conversation I will never forget, about how the doctors think he has mesothelioma (a type of cancer) and that they had to do more tests but it's looking a lot like it.
BOOM! Cancer? CANCER! I couldn't believe what he had said. Not my dad? Nothing like a bit of devastating news to wake you up properly. My brother broke down on the phone to me. I felt completely helpless. This was the first time I had ever heard him cry (apart from that time when we were kids pretending to do boxing and one hit got a little too close to Paul's face and hit his glasses which smashed onto his face. I felt so bad…but this was a different cry like a crushed soul cry). He is definitely not an emotions freeing person, so this told me instantly, dad's situation had changed and not for the better. I wanted to pinch myself and realise that it was only a nightmare…but I wasn't dreaming. This was real and painful. Isn't it weird how someone's emotions on show can tell you everything about a situation versus actual facts on paper.
This is why I love people watching in the airport. There is such a variety of people there. There are people in suits and high heels, eating caviar and smoked salmon right out in the main walk way at a bar, costing them a ridiculous amount of money.
Then there are people about five feet away, lying asleep over three seats in tracksuits and trainers and pulling their coats over them like a blanket. Others are backpackers with their handheld sandwiches and take away coffees, always on the go, walking around looking for things to do because they can't sit still. I'm that person who can't really decide which group I sit in. I dress up with heels (just in case I get upgraded to first class), I have a take away coffee in my hand but I also have my coat over

my legs like a blanket. It always amazes me just how many different kinds of people are around.

Anyway, back to my dad. So what is mesothelioma? Good question. I had no idea when my brother told me at first, it's only because he added cancer at the end of the sentence that I new it was bad. I'm not a doctor but I can tell you all that I found out since it was foreign to me and to everyone I spoke to. Well, it's a type of cancer that's in the lung lining. It can start in the lungs or the abdomen. Dad's was in the lungs. This is called Pleural Mesothelioma. This is the common one although apparently a rare cancer. This type of cancer is connected to being exposed to asbestos, so in fact, if you think about it, it's actually the only cancer that is one hundred percent preventable. Not by dad. No he didn't know that he had breathed some asbestos fibres into his lungs, but if the world was asbestos free, the chances are he would not have got mesothelioma. The asbestos fibres can be breathed in and because they have a hook shape at the end that is how they attach themselves to the lung lining and that's how the cancer starts. I read something the other day that said an asbestos fibre is smaller than a human strand of hair. How the brain can fathom that, I will not know.

It can take quite a few years to develop. We believe my dad was exposed in 1978. It's now 2016 and he is having chemo for the cancer that has just developed. 38 years after being exposed to asbestos and now his life is at risk. The other thing is, the symptoms for this cancer could mean so many other things.

Dad actually had chest pains which made us think it was his heart again as he had a heart attack before. He didn't have the weight loss and loss of appetite till later on. And before anything else he had a cough for ages.

But none of these things make you think cancer straight away. In fact, i think most people just simply think, “It’s just a chest infection”. People questioning whether they had cancer might even think ‘It won’t happen to me’. Well that’s what I thought, and then this happened.
Matthew has always been a wonderfully supportive husband, a lot of the time he might not like or agree with what I want to do but he will completely support me through it. I know, however, it must have taken a lot for him to say for me to go to America to see my dad. We have only ever been away from each other two nights, and only one night at a time. Plus the thought of having to deal with the kids and how they might be missing their mum, since I have never left them longer than a night either. That must have been a worry on his mind.
He said “It’s something you have to do and we will all figure it out”. This made me so happy that he would put everything that was important to me first in his life. That’s how much he loves me. But before I would leave for the trip, there would be a lot more emotions felt, and I was definitely not looking forward to all the tears or the goodbyes.
So I set off planning my trip. I planned when was the best week to leave my family. The best week for childcare. The best week for dad. And I actually planned the perfect week in the end. Mrs Brock at Marlia’s preschool helped out with extra days (thankfully they weren’t full up at that time). And not only that but when I went to talk to her about it, she opened up her office as I was a blubbering mess and took her preschool manager hat off and she was a mum talking to a mum. She calmed me down and made me feel like things would be ok. That is a talent that I completely love in her. My mum was able to help out babysitting sleepovers and cooking for most of the week, my mother and father-in-

law looked after my family on the Sunday with a roast to make Matthew smile (his favourite meal) and dad didn't have a lot of appointments on that week.

I waited till the week before to surprise my dad. I text him saying "how are you?"

He said "I'm ok".

He was either tired or he couldn't think of another way to say 'I'm in a lot of pain but I'm getting through it'. I said "what would make you happier?".

"I am happy" he said to me too quickly that you could tell he was hiding the fact that he actually wasn't, and then I sent him the 'wow' text and waited eagerly for his reply.

"Ok I won't come and visit you next week" The reaction was everything I really wanted.

"Wait what?? Omg! Ange that will be so lovely! Oh I can't wait!"

Then I got even more excited to see him. Perhaps my visit might help him. It might make him feel a bit more happy and feel like he has something to look forward to. I can't wait to start planning what we are going to do together. I have so many ideas and I have no idea where to start. Well I do. Of course I would start with a packing list. I love a good list. I always do this months in advance, it's almost like I can't wait for the trip and it helps to actually start the packing process.

As I look at the piece of paper and think about what I will need, my mind wonders to what i'll be doing with dad. I want so badly to make his week with me the best he's had in a while. I wish I had an abundance of money so I could afford to take dad to all his favourite places and buy him all the things that would make him smile. They say money isn't everything, but I do think money can make some things easier. I don't want to be a millionaire, but i'd like to be able to go to America more often, and i'd like to take my family one day. A dream but hopefully one that will come true. I should have gone back more in the last 8 years. I should have learned the art of saving. Trips to see my dad and brother would have meant more in my book of life than any material things I bought over the years. At least I was hoping  my company on this trip will bring on even the smallest of smiles.

# Chapter 3: Monday…

I washed enough clothes for both kids for the whole week and even wrote Monday through Sunday stickers on each pile. I planned meals for everybody and put meals in the freezer. I packed my bags and before I knew it, the time had come to the very day I was leaving. My mum was taking Marlia to preschool today as to make it not a difficult goodbye send off, but I can already feel the tears building up. All I don't want to do is cry in front of her. I just want to say goodbye, so she doesn't worry, kiss her, and say see you later, so it's an easy transition. But as soon as I go to hug her, I explode into a flood of tears. I can barely talk. She just keeps saying,

"Mummy are you ok? Are you sick?" I'm completely crushed inside at the thought of leaving my family. I reassure her, even though i'm not

convinced, but now you can't take that moment back even though she was fine. It's still a terrible goodbye. She waves goodbye, as do I.
Time is flying and before I know it, it's time to say goodbye to my little boy and husband. Again the floods of tears come running down my cheeks. I jump into Viv's car and the trip starts to feel real.
Viv takes me the scenic route and we enjoy all the wonderful greenery England has an abundance of. Passing a field or two of white fluffy sheep and driving through tunnels made of droopy bendy leafy trees. Hills galore and going past little villages with old churches and small corner shops.
We arrive at the airport and my tummy sinks. I've always been very nervous when I go on aeroplane trips. It's not the trip itself, or the aeroplane itself, it's the lead up to it. The going through security, the finding the right gate to get to, having a bag not too heavy, worrying about being searched. Once I'm flat in the air, I settle, and yet for most people, it's the plane trip itself that everyone is afraid of. I'm here three and a half hours early, but the first lady I get to says I can check in now. So within 5 minutes I have checked my bag in and got my seat number. 35f. Sounds like a shoe size from Clarks. At least it's an aisle seat, making it easier to get up to the toilet or just for a wander every hour. I go through to the big shopping and food court lounge where you wait to find out your gate number.
It's huge. Full of rich expensive shops and restaurants galore. All the restaurants seem more expensive than I remember them to be. I sit down and listen to some music. As I sit there, I think about all the fun things I will do with my dad, and how even though my brother says he can't walk far, part of me is thinking I can change that. I think about what I'm going to say to him as soon as I see him and I feel a tear building up. I think

about something else to stop it from slipping out of my eye, it doesn't work so I walk around for a bit and stop to look at the map of the airport. A couple stopped next to me. I overheard the woman say,
"Everything is too posh here, all I want is a cheap burger!"
This struck me as a funny thing to say. When you go on holiday (or at least this is what I think), you don't think, 'let's go for the cheapest meal out'. That's usually on the way home, when you are running out of money. You want something to start the holiday off with a bang, something tasty, something almost lavish, and yet all they wanted was a cheap burger. Cheap and cheerful. Probably not the best food but fairly inexpensive, instant. I don't know if that's the American coming out of me, (you see I was born there but now live in sunny England in a small town called Worthing) but that seems like a very British way of looking at a meal. However I know there are plenty of Americans that can appreciate a it too.
So I board the plane and I sit next to a young twenties something girl. She was wearing a loose blue cotton jumper and skinny jeans, I noticed this because I always wear something comfortable when on a plane trip (apart from this trip as I was hoping on getting upgraded) because you are basically sitting for the longest time in what is not more room that a seat in a car, and jeans to me are never something I would choose for comfort. She had small round shaped glasses on and long mousy brown hair that rested on her shoulders like a cat curled up on a sofa. She put her rucksack in the overhead compartment and her lightweight coat and then buckled herself into her seat. She is sitting with what I thought was her much older father, but after an extensive chat with her about her 10 week vacation to America, it sounds more like the gentleman is her boyfriend.

Shock horror. I don't change my facial expression when it finally clicks, but deep down all I'm thinking is 'I haven't even been on the plane 5 minutes and I already have two people to entertain me the whole way!'. I don't have any problem with people having 10 years difference or less but more than that is crazy in my opinion. You can't have much in common, and while you might be wanting to do lots of exciting things in 10 years time, your partner is probably needing to slow down.

This girl went on to say they had rented a flat for their 10 week trip. This sounds amazing, but what I can't understand is how can anyone afford this? My trip is one week long and I'm either staying with my dad or a friend, meaning no cost. But still I have to pay for the ticket, food, petrol for my ride to pick me up from the airport, souvenir money and then money for the taxis to and from the airport in England. I can't even imagine adding a 10 week rent cost on top of that. Maybe they had saved up for a couple of years, or maybe they have a money tree. Who knows? Something else that shocks me…

On aeroplanes now you can get ice-cream. How crazy is that? I'm sitting in my seat (My friend previously warned me there could possibly be some on board) and in front I hear,

"Would you like an ice-cream sir?"

I look in front and the man is opening up a fruit lolly with sprinkles on it! So I guess it's not really the kind of ice-cream I like, I'm more of a mint chocolate chip kind of girl, but the fact you can have ice-cream on a plane is amazing. Food on planes has come a long way in the 8 years I haven't been doing international travel. There was also promise of popcorn, but I didn't see any of that this trip. Perhaps next time.

Even the movie system is 100% better than it was all those years ago. It's a much easier way to get your movie. You can start it straight away, pause it easily and it continuously tells you how much time you have on your trip. I can't tell you how much I adore this. I'm a clock watcher on a plane. I like to know just how long I have till I get somewhere. It's a phenomenal set-up and it just makes viewing things much more accessible. It's not just your standard 6 movies either. There's loads of tv and music. Needless to say you can't get bored even on a 12 hour flight like I did. The only thing they need to improve on is the seating. I guess if you have a lot of money you can go into business or first class. Economy is awful, no matter how many good movies are playing, no matter how much free alcohol or ice-cream you have and hot food, you are still going to ache like nothing else when you get off. That really puts me off going back on a plane again. Obviously not hugely off putting because in my head I'm already planning my next trip over. It's a bit like giving birth. Not always easy, but most people are eager to go for another.

The long flight is finally over. I'm glad to be getting off the aeroplane and walking in normal air. I get through to get my bags and security really fast. This really was something, because I had heard security was becoming slower and slower to go through, and after a really long flight, the last thing you really want is to be waiting in a long line for hours. My phone doesn't work because I can only use wifi and there isn't any here. This makes me feel really anxious about the rest of my trip. It's the weirdest thing, I almost feel naked without the use of my phone. It's not just a phone to me, it's a clock, a calendar, a computer and my main communicator. It will be good to have some time away from it.

I call my friend Heather who is picking me up. Heather is my best friend's mum and i've adopted her as my American mum. She always has a big smile and she has taught me a lot over the years so i'm looking forward to seeing her. The phone call will cost me a bomb I think to myself, but shrug it off as I have no choice and I walk out of the airport. I breath in the night air…I am home. Matthew hates whenever I refer to America as my home. Obviously wherever he is…That is home to me. But when I'm in America, there's an instant feeling of home to me. It's a bit like when someone makes you roast potatoes like your mum used to. The smell, the taste, the way your house fills up with remembered feelings…that's how I feel when I first breathe in the air and feel the warmth of California rest on my shoulders. When I pass a palm tree or drive past a popular supermarket. When I walk around the mall with all the many clothes shops I love or the smell of hot tacos with spicy salsa verde.

In England my home feelings are my husband's skin and body spray smell. His beard when he goes to kiss me straight from a shower and his arms when he wraps them around me. It's his cute freckle that sits on his right earlobe and the way he laughs at stuff I don't find funny. It's my kids morning kisses and cuddles and their "I love you's". It's the love look in Matthew's eyes and the feel of safe when he holds me through thunder and lightning. I think people must have more than one 'home' feeling or place. I don't think everybody would say the house they live in is the only home they feel they have. It would be interesting to find out.

One of my favourite homes away from home is at my friend Susan's house. She offered to have me stay with her when I first discussed going on this trip. I know what you are thinking, I'm here only for a week, I should be staying with my dad. People have already said to me, I know it's not a holiday for you…but for me, this was kind of a holiday for me. For me, I was expecting to have a bit of fun with my dad. Make happy memories, enjoy our time together, because as morbid as this sounds, this could be the last time (well I think one part of my head is thinking that anyway, the rest of me completely is believing he is so strong he will blow this cancer out of him through the clouds and out of sight). I also have a lot of friends who I would love to see as the last time I was here was 8 years ago. It's so hard to do both in just one week. I also need to see my uncle, aunt, cousins and grandma. I said to her I would stay with her in the middle of the week and one more day, but the rest at dad's. Thinking about all the people I need to see makes me think about all the people I have left behind.

My wonderful husband that I love and adore.

My beautiful kids that I can't bare to be away from.

My mum who I talk to everyday.

It's such a tug of war. I'm the rope in the middle and I'm being pulled from America to England and England to America. So what is the answer? I have no idea. It's something I work on everyday. I don't think I will ever be content in either country. That's just how it will have to be.

I look around at the many people getting picked up and all the people sitting on suitcases still waiting. The big red truck my friend Heather was driving, drove straight past me. Thankfully she stopped just ahead so I walked briskly towards her (well as best I could with high heels on). Heather sees me, gets out of the car and gives me the warmest of welcome hugs. I feel happy now. I get in the car and we reminisce about old times and this is when I stop suddenly and say,

"Sorry but I'm suddenly aware of my very English accent"

It kind of sounds like I'm putting a thick English accent on, but I completely am not. We both laugh. She asks me if I am hungry…I was secretly hoping she would ask me this. I instantly answer yes knowing that a specific burger joint that is only in California is a hop skip and a jump away. She suggests we go there and I happily except. We take it back to hers and I devour it. It's just as good as it was 8 years ago. The toasted bun, the tasty meat, the fresh salad. I'm in heaven. Suddenly there's a knock at the door. It can't possibly be Paul, I have only just got here and was hoping on having at least an hour with Heather.

It's Paul. I feel almost sad but I realise that he has come a long way and I need to go with him. Heather and Tillman (Heather's husband) say a prayer for us. We hug and then I leave for another hour and a half car journey home. We get almost into my home town and Paul turns to me and says,

"Do you like wings?"

I looked at him and wanted to say yes to make him happy and start off the right way, but thinking about all the bones and skin I knew I couldn't eat it.

"No, not really"

He pauses. "Ok well I'm hungry so do you mind if we stop here?"

I look at the time…it's 11pm. On a regular day I only see this time at night because one of the kids have woken me up. I was so tired from all the travelling and wanted nothing more than to hit the pillow and fall fast asleep.

"Not at all"

We walked into this place that didn't look too special to be honest. Just really a fast food chain with a couple of tables and chairs, one of those big menu signs behind the counter and someone taking the orders. He ordered his wings and whilst in a daze of sleep deprivation I overheard the words 'lemon pepper glaze'. I had to try it. We sat down and when it arrived I was in complete shock. These were not wings in the ordinary sense. They were basically top quality crunchy chicken nuggets. They had a lemon pepper liquid on them, but this didn't make them any less crunchy, and to be honest with you, the crunch is what I love the most. We had a ranch dressing to dunk them in. My goodness. All my head was thinking was I must have more. They are so addictive. It didn't take us long to finish the whole plate.We got back in the car and headed home. I knew I had to make time to go back this week.

Paul started to drive and all I could think about was, is dad going to look awful? Will I cry when I see him? I don't want to upset him with any of my reactions. I want him to light up like he always used to after not seeing me for a while. When we arrived I walked in, put my bags down, and there he was standing with a cane in the lounge.

It's been 17 months since I've seen my dad, and so much has changed. The moment I saw my dad after not seeing him for so long, I knew I had lost the big bouncy personality that was my dad. The dad I grew up with. To be honest with you, he had changed a lot in the last 3 years, but there was a dramatic change in the last 17 months.

That person, that as a kid till I was at least 17, I completely idolised, well, I still idolised him now but back then even more, he had changed a lot in my 20's and then 3 years ago he came to visit me just after my little girl was born and he was fun again, but still not like he used to be. Then 17 months ago when he came to visit again he changed yet again...but not for the better. Everywhere he went his phone was with him. He would be on it even while eating dinner. While we were talking. During a film.It was like his body was here but his mind was somewhere else, and the quality time I had craved for was not all I thought it would be unfortunately.

I later found out it was because he was doing stocks and shares and because of the time difference, he had to go on during our day time. Money was his big focus this trip. He wasn't relaxed at all. I felt like we didn't really make any real memories this trip. This was sad for me because something inside of me was telling me he was not going to be back for a long time. But then when I saw him this time, he had lost 40/50 pounds, (Dad had always had a big belly and a round face and my favourite were his chunky square shaped fingers) he was walking with a cane and he was a lot slower. He wasn't occupied by his phone and he wasn't worried if the stocks had gone up or down. You could see he actually just wanted to enjoy every minute with me.

What a difference, in a good way, to the man I had seen not that long ago. I was sad I only had 6 days with the new/old dad. Even more sad that I had booked some of that time with friends which would make our time shorter, but it was something I needed to do.

First conversation I had with my dad after not seeing him for a year and a half, was not the heart to heart I was hoping for. It wasn't how great it was to see me. It actually ended up being randomly (although not random if you knew my dad) about how he had changed all the lights in the house to more energy efficient light bulbs. Anybody who knows my dad knows this is typically him. He can talk his socks off about anything for hours…but it is usually something that you are not interested in. I was expecting a wonderful deep and meaningful conversation…nope…it was about energy efficient light bulbs.

My brother touched my shoulder and I knew this was the moment I was going to meet his Korean, shy new wife, who didn't know a lot of English. I was nervous and wanted this moment to be perfect. It was more of a 'hi' and 'bye' since it was so late at night. But somehow the way she said 'hi' made me feel like she instantly liked me. Or is that just the way Korean people speak? Either way, I felt a little less stressed.

My brother showed me to my room and gave me the code for the house internet and a key to the front door and then said goodnight. I got into the sheets and covered up with the thin duvet and felt comfy. I called Matthew just to hear his voice for 2 minutes before I fell fast asleep. I could tell he wanted to talk more, but even though my heart was saying 'let's talk for another hour' my body was saying 'night night'. I wanted to get enough sleep in because I knew I would be up early due to jet lag and also wanted the day to be wonderful for all of us. I was excited to have some proper time with dad and to make him smile.

# Chapter 4: Tuesday…

So this morning started with a wake up at 4:30am due to jet lag and probably a bit of excitement to start the day. I get up and go downstairs and put the coffee on. Apart from this morning when I had no idea how to use the machine and no one got up till 9! Imagine being up that early and not getting even a mouthful of coffee for hours…this is literally one of my worst nightmares. I looked in all the cupboards for instant coffee or ground coffee, but found none. Not even a kettle. I saw the coffee machine, but I really had no idea how to use it, so I thought I would just wait for someone to get up. As soon as Paul got up and walked downstairs, I jumped up and I think I said something to the effect of "dude…make the coffee now!"

The machine my dad has is the best coffee machine I have ever used. It so simple. You choose a coffee pod, put it in, pull the handle down, then press the start button. And then the most amazing mug of coffee appears right in front of you. So fresh, so strong and so quick. This literally sets you up for the day perfectly. Not only that, but later on I found out you can actually buy medicine pods to put in it so you can make a kind of hot lemon medicine drink. How genius is that? I fell in love with it.

My machine at home is good but this was far ahead anything I had ever seen. This is followed by a slice of toast, wholemeal of course, but none of the wholemeal over here tastes like cardboard. In fact it's sweet and doughy. I can't get enough of it. I never thought I would ever say that about wholemeal. All around the kitchen there are so many different machines. But in one corner it's completely devoted to coffee. My dad's coffee machine is amazing. It takes pods and it makes coffee shop equivalent quality coffee. There are tons of these pods. Flavoured coffee (no doubt these are my brothers pods) a couple of the odd medium roast and a couple of the dark roast pods. And then there are a box of what must be my dad's favourite since there are so many of them. Peat's dark roast. He's obviously gone through a number of pods and finally found one he loves. I on the other hand love starbucks medium roast. I also quite like the one that's called donut shop medium roast.

When dad gets up in morning you can just see he is a creature of habit. First he gets out a mug, usually the massive tall green ones he's kept that we used to have when I lived here, grabs a peat's pod and puts it in. Then a bowl and spoon for his cereal of choice (although mostly a shredded wheat type) but it does have to be a specific make. Apparently not all shredded wheat taste that good. I have to say this true with cornflakes, so maybe he is on to something.

He sits down and always takes a mouthful of his coffee first. The reaction he gives after that first mouthful, is much like mine…happiness. We are set up for the day and nothing is more joyful than that moment. My dad and I don't have blood in our veins, we have strong coffee filtering through us and keeping us going. This was his routine 8 years ago, and it hasn't changed a bit. I then experienced complete joy. Having that first shower after you have been in a plane for almost 12 hours and then in a car for almost 2 hours. I felt fresh again!

My dad has this shower that has such power to it. If I were to tell you the food equivalent of mine at home was like a cheap drive-through burger and my dad's is top of the range, organic steak, the type that turns up in a brioche bun, you would know how wonderful it was.

Both my dad and my brother just kept saying have a shower, twice a day if you want after I expressed my love for it. My brain reeked of my 8 years spent in England because I immediately thought about saving on the water meter. I think it seems to me the only time people in America really think about saving water is that crazy time of the year, summer, when there's a hosepipe ban. At home we tend to have showers and only once a day to save money. I love a bubble bath, but there's no point in having one unless it's really full up, right up to your chin and that would be too much water.

Other things that keep you going, specially when you are away from home, and are a real big comfort are:

1. A comfy bed
2. A good night's sleep
3. Skype…and the most important…
4. Good food…or food that makes you smile!

Everyone has food in common with each other. For me, it's all about the food that is fattening. Burgers, pizza, donuts. You know the kind that you just look at it and you know you are going to gain weight as soon as it hits your lips. Bacon cheesy burgers, overloaded cheesy pizza and hot glazed ring donuts. Luckily I was visiting America, so i was pretty safe in knowing I would have all these things.

I headed out to Granary Square to meet up with another one of my friends. She is the sweetest girl and possibly the only person the same size as me (5'1) and the other thing about her is that she is always happy and smiling. I don't think I have ever seen her sad. We talked about my life, her life, my babies, babies she wants, and then I had to go back to do something fun with dad.

I bought my dad a scrapbook whilst still in England. I wanted to take over a project for us to do to give us a fun time. In my head I imagined us to have thousands of bright coloured paints everywhere, aprons and projects flying out of heads. I thought there would be smiles all around and it would take his mind off all the things bothering him. I was wrong. I gave him the scrapbook with pictures I had printed off for him and colours in hopes that he might do some sort of an amazing collage. He opened it up and looked a little lost. This upset me, but I didn't let him know. I didn't show my emotions, he didn't need that. He needed anything to brighten his day, not darken it with a black cloud.

My old dad would never had been lost with paper and colours. He would find it an adventure. He would inspire me. But instead he just kept saying "What do I do? Where do I start? How do I do this?" Which completely stunned me to no end. Most people would have asked these normal questions, but my dad was the most creative person I knew. His whole being was a colourful sunset full of brightly coloured fireworks. He was my very own Picasso and everything he put his paintbrush to turned into the most beautiful piece of artwork made entirely of dreams and hopes and visions.

When I was younger, we used to go to one of those places where you paint pottery together. My dad would always make the best things and I would always want to steal his ideas. This man sat in front of me was far from that old vision of mine. Art was one of our big things we used to bond over. Give us a blank canvas and some paint and a masterpiece would be made. We loved all things creative. I couldn't understand who or what had sucked all the creativity vibe right out of him. I'm very sure it was the cancer. Cancer has a way of eating away at everything that makes you you. I think even if you beat cancer, it still takes a part of you that you can never get back. It's such a horrible thing for someone to get. My heart literally sinks when I hear someone has it.

Eventually he puts pen to paper but you could see the stress on his face to produce something good. I actually had brought an activity that had made the situation worse rather than brighten the mood. This made me so sad, and I longed to have my dad back with me.

I had arranged to meet up with my friends in granary square, a little area of shops not too far from the house in beautiful Valencia, this morning. This is mainly because I know I can walk there from the paseos down my dad's road. Pasaos, if you didn't know, are basically an easy straight walk, through beautiful pathways with trees either side. There are so many in Santa Clarita. This is great for me specially since I don't drive.

I walk down the paseos as it's a beautiful sunny day in October. It's currently 80 some odd degrees and i'm wearing a cardy. Why am I doing that? Mainly because it's in October and I thought it would be cold, but half way through this walk I take it off. The warmth on my face and shoulders is amazing. I miss it. Getting up to the sunshine is what I love best. There's something about getting up when it's sunny that makes all of you shine. Not just on the outside but on the inside too. Although the paseos are just literally one scenic walkway, that doesn't have a huge amount of flowers, it's still a beautiful way to get to the shops. It's quiet and serene. You always have someone greet you with a big smile and a cheerful 'good morning/afternoon'. It doesn't matter how old the person is, young or old, they just do it. If you were to do this over here, in England, people would look at you like you are weird. Ok maybe they wouldn't if you were old, I guess, but they would if you were young. It's almost robotic in a way because the person walking towards you could be speed walking or going for a run, but as soon as they look up and see you, it's "Good morning" finished with a big smile. Then they instantly go back to whatever they were doing. However robotic this ritual is, it is still warming to the heart. It makes me smile and I know it makes my day a bit brighter. I'm sure I'm not the only one who thinks this, and I bet if this made a lot of people feel like this, imagine what would happen if everyone did it in every country.

These two friends I'm meeting, I've know for practically the same amount of time give or take a year or two. Lily I met first. She was my partner in crime. My beautiful friend who I got to work with. We had so much fun together. It didn't feel like work with her around. Coming from Cuba, Lily was all kinds of wonderful. She had a way of telling you exactly what she thought and she was always right and exactly to the point. Lily has the biggest smile a person could have laying on her face, without using cosmetic surgery…because she certainly didn't believe in that. Leah was a parent of one of the children in my class. Her daughter was possibly my funniest personality that enter any of my classes. She was so sweet as was her mum and that's how we started being friends. This mum was so young looking and so in shape even after having 2 kids. I wanted to look like her when I met her back when I didn't have any kids, and I still want her youthful looks and it's over 10 years now since we met.

We met up at a very popular coffee house. The type you see on every corner in America. We got coffee and caught up with how life had been treating all of us. I had noticed Lily seemed a lot slower in doing things that I remembered she was 8 years before. I don't know if it's because dads diagnosis, but it made me worry about her. I had about an hour with them and then it was time to go. Leah gave me a lift home and I grabbed some time with dad. He's watching TV. What's new. He turns it off and turns to me to talk. We talk about his current favourite show. Hawaii 5 0. He loves it, in fact he cant get enough of it. I haven't seen him this interested in a programme since the days of Star Trek.

After we have this long talk about the 2 main characters he tells me he needs to go to sleep so he goes upstairs to have a nap. Paul then takes me to the mall to meet my other friends I said I would meet today. Noelle and Barb. Noelle and I have known each other for at least 15 years. We used to work at a school together. She worked in the class next to me. She was the tallest teacher and I think I was the shortest. She has these massive amazing eyes, the kind a Disney princess would have and a beautiful heart to match. She is such a sweet woman who loves nothing more than making people happy. She has 2 gorgeous children who look like mini ones of her and her husband.

Barb I've known for the same amount of time and from the same school.

She has the most wonderful head of hair I wish I could have. Thick and shiny and I know if she were to walk in the wind it would suddenly change into one of those slow motion movements with her hair beautifully rippling in a rhythmic way. She has a big smile that makes you want to smile right back at her. She is an amazing lady to me. Since I moved over here she had 2 children and her life has been turned upside down. The thing is, both her children have lots of health problems. They both have something called "Primary Immunodeficiency Disease" which means they have to go to hospital about an hour away every other week to have blood infusions. Her son in addition has "Crohn's Disease" too. This will happen for the rest of their lives. And that is just on good weeks. Sometimes they are so sick they can't go to school. Every time I think of Barb, which is most days, I think about how blessed I am that both my children are healthy and have no health problems.

So I'm waiting outside the mall to meet my friends and I realise that my brother didn't get a reply back from my friends, saying whether or not we could change the meeting spot to the mall, and because my phone doesn't work and my brother had dropped me off and had to hurry to take my dad to an appointment, there was no way to get a hold of anyone. So I look around and I see a lady with a phone near her. She's sitting outside the mall chomping on a burger that quite frankly I was drooling over. I ask her if she knows where the nearest payphone was. She replied in a really thick American accent, "Payphones? No we don't have any of those here" I'm pretty sure they do, but I'm also sure she has never had the joys of using one.

But she offers me the use of her mobile phone and without any hesitation I said yes please and called my friends. My friends were on their way so I hang up the phone and give it back to her. The lady and I then have a long discussion on how long I was staying and what are the best foods to taste and as quick as that, she leaves and I never see her again. It's funny how you make friends with strangers never to see them after that. Noelle and Barb arrive and we enter the mall and head straight to the food court. I go to the corn dog place and my friends go get a salad. I order a beef corn dog, a lemonade and a funnel cake. There are two people ahead of me and two people waiting behind me and there's a boy on his own manning the whole station. I can already see he has made a couple of mistakes and he hasn't even come to my order yet. I can also see the sheer panic in his face because he doesn't know which order to fix first. Then his co-worker returns back from what must have been her break and she can tell everything is messed up and it's going to be ages to catch up. More people arrive and ask for food. You can tell she's not interested in working at all, she just wants to run out, but she obviously needs the job, because she is keeping her cool and saying just the right things to the customers whilst fixing the problems one by one. At this point the boy just keeps walking back and forth like he's pretending to work but really has no idea what he is doing.

Whenever the girl has her back turned to do the orders and the customers can't see (although I did) she's rolling her eyes at the boy and huffing and puffing like she's had enough. It's such a shame because the corndog was amazing. I don't know how they get the hotdog inside so hot but still juicy whilst the outer layer is crunchy the whole way round but fluffy on the inside. Tasty! Probably my favourite things to eat in the mall. The funnel cake on the other hand wasn't all I had imagined it to be. Parts of it were crispy but other parts were chewy. It mostly tasted of powdered sugar and nothing else. I would not order this again, even though everyone says how great it was, and you can't go home without having a funnel cake. I would have been happier with a double portion of corn dog. I had a lovely chat with my friends and then it was time to go home. My lovely friend Barb drove me home. As I hugged her goodbye I wondered when I would get to see her next. I so miss her friendship. I walked inside and dad was sat in front of the tv again. I sat down with him and we had a random moment. Dad actually asked me a question and wasn't rambling on about stuff you had no interest in.

"What book are you reading now?" I had no idea he even knew I liked to read. I had brought a book for the plane trip, 'Life of Pi", and at this point dad got really excited. Finally! I thought to myself. He said he had seen the film and he owned it. I said I had not seen it so he went to get it so we could watch it. Of course it wasn't going to be a simple 'put the dvd in the player and watch it'. No dad didn't have a dvd player. So he got his laptop and speakers, and started the half an hour fiddle of getting it all to work together, so we could watch the movie and actually hear it. It was almost automatic, as soon as he hit the play button, that's when he decided it was the best time to talk about those freaking energy light bulbs again. I will never understand why he does that. At this point I am doing three different things. Yes I can multitask. I'm watching the movie out of the corner of my eye, pretending to listen to dad's story of the wonder lights and texting my brother who is upstairs to ask him

"Why must dad tell me unimportant things while I'm trying to watch this movie??"

It's funny because all I have wanted to do is sit and chat with him, but the moments he does, all I want him to do is be quiet. I must get better at being patient with him in these situations and at least little properly to what he has to say.

This evening we all have been invited to my uncle's house for dinner. It used to be my grandma's house when I lived here, but they all live here now. I walk into the house and I instantly feel 17 again. Stonefire dinner- the usual. All the same faces, just a little older, minus my grandma as she is in hospital again. My auntie and uncle are divorced and yet we are all sitting at the dinner table. That house is a time warp. The sofas might be different but everything else is the same. There's even that old peoples scent wafting in the air, even though we have barbequed meats and garlic mash coming into the house. The food was just as delicious as the last time I had it…8 years ago. Nobody does mash potato as good as this place…well maybe just one. My gorgeous friend Becky has a beautifully talented mum that makes amazing mash. Every time I went over to her house, when we were teens, I hoped she would be making that for us. It's the type that is so creamy but still has a couple of lumps in it for added texture. People tend to want just straight creamy mash but that's the type I hate. The lumps make it taste much more real. Like you know it's been made with real potatoes. And that's what makes it pure gold for me. We look at old pictures of me and Paul and the rest of the family that are still up on the shelves, and I half fall asleep because the jetlag is horrific. My head actually feels like I can't hold it up anymore. My eyelids feel like some sort of magnet is pulling them closed. It's at this point we decide we have to go. We leave and I head straight to bed.

# Chapter 5: Wednesday…

Today we had a couple of visitors, starting with my dads 'oldest' friend, meaning he was a friend for the longest time and not that he was very old. Chris and dad met on the ships and both met their wives around the same time and have stayed friends ever since. He brought dad some gorgeous oranges because dad loves freshly squeezed orange juice. When they are together you can just tell they like each other for who they are. There's mutual respect and a kind of love that's almost a replica of being brothers. Their friendship will most definitely last a lifetime. He couldn't stay very long because he lives quite a distance away, but a visit from him has really lifted dads spirits and that's the best thing to see from him.

Dad's lawyer came over this afternoon. Fresh out of high school, ok that was a bit extreme, college…but probably graduated the youngest in his class. Arrived in an expensive suit and swanky shoes, you know the kind, pointy and so shiny it reminds me of uncle festers head, you can see your reflection on them. He walked in very casually, like he had walked into thousands of mesothelioma cancer ridden houses, to start a battle to win against the people who made this disease fester inside people's bodies. He sat down and took out his notebook and a pen and then we had a casual chat about the two current people up for being president…as you do. To be fair, it lightened the mood and broke the ice a bit. He then ever so often asked questions regarding how dad had come in contact with the asbestos. This was all quite hard because it had been so long ago trying to track down all the information proved hard, but we got there in the end. At one point he said something that hit me like a ton of bricks, although I'm pretty sure I didn't show it.

"Now I need to point out, as horrible as this sounds, if you were to pass away, you would only receive about 10% of what you could have got…"

Pass away? My dad isn't going to pass away! Why would he say that? Why would he bring up such a horrible thing? I looked at him and inside almost laughed at him, but also completely wanted to shout his head off for even bringing those words into this house. I was so angry at him, but kept my cool. My dad is not going to die, so they are going to have to pay the full amount, for messing up his body and making it so he can't even work! You fight for us and you get it done, I thought to myself. And even if he did pass away, which he's not going to, surely that's when the family could use the help for funeral costs and paying the remainder of the mortgage and just getting through life? It doesn't change the fact that he got cancer because of that deadly material somebody decided to use in his workplace. Are they saying that it's not as important to win the case if

he dies? That's so messed up. I tried to not get too angry about it whilst he was with us, but it's just ridiculous.
The time passed quickly and then he had to leave. We said our goodbyes and I really hoped he would do his best for us. I mean…that was his job.
Today I am going to see my mum and dad's oldest friends, Carla and Fernando. If you want to know what the definition of true friendship is, look in the dictionary and a big picture of them would be there. They are so loving and caring towards us all, and now that Paul and I are older, we actually look at them as our friends too. Paul's actually the lucky one because they also happen to be his godparents. I so wish they had been mine. It's actually a fun thing to have these people as friends, as they knew our mum and dad before we were old enough to properly know them. The other thing is, Carla is an amazing cook. She makes amazing Mexican food, but we wouldn't be having that today as it was a quick visit. We decided to have some yummy Chinese takeaway instead.
The moment they arrived I could feel the warmth of their love for us radiate the room. Big smiles filled the living room and everyone was really happy for a while. The weather was beautiful so Paul suggested we ate outside. I took some spray outside and went to clean the glass table. As I clean the right hand corner I saw something black shine a patch of red to me. I quickly walked indoors and walked over to my brother in the kitchen and whispered in his ear
"Is it black widows that have red on their backs?"
He turned to me, asked me where I saw it and then I took him to see it.
He looked closely, stood up and then said
"Yea we're not going to eat outside, let's stick to the lounge". Crazy!
We ate and shared stories. We reminisced about the old days and our

favourite foods we have eaten together. Carla and I took pictures and before long it was time for their visit to come to an end. We hugged them goodbye and hoped it wouldn't be too long before we would all be together again. Before coming here I was so stressed with lots of things and on top of it I had stress about my dad having cancer, I had stressed about my children's book launch, stress about leaving my family, stress with worrying about childcare, but it's funny what stress can do to you when you finally relax. I know the exact moment I started to relax. It wasn't the moment I landed, it wasn't the morning after my first night here. I would say it was once all my friends had arrived to the evening meal we had planned on the Wednesday. I relaxed through that night as well because I was able to sleep the whole night through in a really comfy bed too. The next morning, even more relaxing. I woke up to the perfect mug of coffee and a great chat with a friend. It was great because when I stay with my brother, he usually doesn't wake up till 8 or 9. My friend Susan, everyday, wakes up at 5. This is perfect for someone who has jet lag, because I wake up around 3, so it's not long before I have human contact. So most of the stress had gone but in the back of my mind, I still had a few worries about my dad but all in all he wasn't looking too bad, so I started to feel good. Unbeknown to me, 3 days later I would have shingles because of actually relaxing, and now this illness could take over my life for the next 4-5 weeks. My husband's client still has pain 2 years down the line. As bad as this sounds, and I definitely value my health…it was worth it, and I don't regret taking some time out to see my dad and feel like he's going to be ok. He's going to beat this awful thing called cancer. It would mean I could come home and not be constantly thinking if he's going to die, or if the chemo isn't going to work. Yes the cancer had taken part of my dad…but not all of him. He still had his smile. Once that was gone, I would have to start to worry. But for now I would enjoy this time with my friends.

The meal I had arranged with friends was really enjoyable. A bunch of lovely ladies I used to work with and haven't seen for 8 years. One of the teachers in the next room from me, Susan who was the schools admin, the director and my old boss, and my assistant teacher. It was just nice to have some time for me, where I wasn't constantly reminded about dad and his cancer. We talked about all our current jobs or interests and we laughed. I feel like ever since that day in April, I've been so serious and stressed that it was a welcomed release.

We ate the beautiful meal and I had a very large jug of pink lemonade I might add. I had momentarily forgotten I was in America and order a drink that I probably could have shared with the whole table.

We then said our goodbyes, each said we would keep in touch via social media, and then with a goodbye that felt more like when a coworker leaves work on a Friday, but you know you'll see them on a Monday, Susan and I went home to take in the beautiful evening. What would tomorrow bring me?

Something great I hoped. But even with such a lovely end of the day, in the back of my mind, I still was worried for tomorrow and what it would look like. Going to sleep would still be hard but at least I had a break from being me today.

# Chapter 6: Thursday…

The second chemo session, I happened to be in the country for and was fortunate to see it go through. Not only that but I was able to see the effects of the new steroids my dad had to go on. These are much stronger steroids. He has to take them the day before, the day of and the day after chemo. The night before Paul told me he heard dad making lots of noises in the middle of the night. Apparently he was fixing his computer. This was the first sign I should have noticed, I should have wondered why he wasn't so tired like all the other evenings. Dad would have done this as the norm before the cancer, but definitely not since. Thursday morning I woke up thinking, I wonder how this is going to go. I wonder if today is going to be horrible…and it wasn't horrible, but definitely stressful.

Dad came downstairs and he was doing everything really fast and I didn't even think there was a faster way of doing a coffee pod machine...but dad proved me wrong this particular morning. He actually seemed like he was on speed. Rushing around, chatting a mile a minute, eating cereal like he hadn't eaten in 3 weeks. He was really worried he had lost a pot of pills and was crazy looking for them. Paul reminded him that he stays in the house the whole time so they can't be lost but misplaced. He was still really worried and had panic all over his face. Paul told me he was up till 4am just doing crazy things, and the whole change in him was due to these new steroids that he has to take for 3 days. The change was so drastic it was like a toy that's batteries were running out and then swapping them for a new pack of Duracell plus and pressing the non-stop button.

Walking down to the chemo session it didn't feel like I imagined it to be. I was walking down this hallway. This pristine, glistening white clean hallway...something you could eat your dinner off of. You enter this room with smiling happy kind looking nurses, who don't look scary at all. In fact they look like they would be my friend outside the hospital. My dads chemo nurses, *Kate* and *Chloe*, (*names have been changed here*) both have very big smiley faces, and you can just tell they are doing this job because they want to care for people. This should be a mandatory skill when applying for this job. The ambience in the hospital is so friendly. Everybody greets my dad as if they have been friends for years. For me, a close family member to him, it is such a comfort to see this and know he is being cared for by people who really just want to do their best.

There's 3 reclining chairs with dividing curtains and in my dad's own words "It's like a spa experience for me", because he says, he gets to lay back in this comfortable reclining chair, he has a warming blanket on him, he wears his headphones and listens to music, and it's "just so comfortable". This goes on for 4 and a half hours. He can catch up on his sleep or finish reading a book. To me, it reminded me of those business class airline seats...probably because I had not long come off a plane. Either way, it's a much better view on chemo then I ever thought I would have. The day he had his chemo session was actually quite a nice day. Dad was laughing and joking with the nurses, as was Paul and I. He looked happy and for the most part, there was only one other woman having chemo, who slept for the majority of the time. It's a couple of days after this that things change. So I ended up feeling quite happy I got to watch this process. We even skyped with my home group whilst he was in the chair and he joking with them too. It almost felt like everything I had seen about chemo was a lie.

Now I know this is in America, but I presume it can't be that different from everywhere else. Chemo is chemo everywhere right? I'm fully aware there are different types of chemo. I'm just glad my dad is living through this one. From what I hear, it's fine the day you have it done, but a couple of days after through to about half way of a 21 day cycle it's rough. When I arrived he was almost at the end of the 21 day cycle, so he was at his best for the most part that I was there.

Walking around, making coffee and breakfast for himself, and happy in himself. All things I was not expecting. The only difference was that he was very thin and walking with a cane. He had chemo on the Thursday and by Saturday morning, the day I was leaving, he wasn't well and 100% different. And apparently even worse on the Sunday. He couldn't get up

without help. He couldn't make his coffee or breakfast…and he didn't want it either.
At lunchtime on Thursday, my brother and I went to his work and had lunch. Dad couldn't eat till chemo was done and we would need to eat before then. We sat there eating tacos and churros from my favourite place and suddenly fell into an in-depth chat about religion. What he believed in, what I believed in. I'm not actually saying who is right, but I don't understand how two people who lived in the same house, in the same family, can have such different beliefs. Especially when It comes to someone so close to us. This operation my dad is supposed to have could be fatal. Nobody knows how it will go. Either way, we both know, no matter how you do things, no matter how much you worry, nothing will change that. Cancer in itself is something you really don't have any control over. My dad has told me that a number of times and how much that scares him. What will be, will be.
Anyone, who gets told they have cancer and then has to fight through it, because you have to fight, must be scared. It's a proper mean illness. My mum's friend has never really been the same since she had it. She didn't die from it, but a little piece of her did die. She will never get that back and we will forever miss that part of her.
When dad had finished he was hungry and the one thing he wanted was a turkey club sandwich. So we went to a bakery on the corner. I ordered his sandwich and while I was waiting I could hear the pumpkin spiced muffin whispering to me,
"Don't leave me here, pick me up and eat me". I quickly asked for one to go but cheekily started to eat it whilst I was waiting. It was one of those really amazing ones that has a crunchy muffin top and soft moist bottom. I

finished it before I even stepped out towards the car and I was glad I listened to the muffin. We got home and I put dad's (expensive at $9.85! I can get a whole dinner with that!?!?!) sandwich on a plate. He asked for only half and to put the other half in the fridge for another day...another day? Surely the bread will become soggy making it taste horrible? Then I remembered that dads taste buds are ruined through chemo and I proceeded to pop it in the fridge. He ate it saying how yummy it was and thanked me a million times which made me feel like I had finally done something right.

Dad put the tv on again, as he was so used to doing when he's in the house. He said what do you want to watch? To be honest, I didn't really want to watch tv. I wanted to go for a walk or sit outside, but apparently he couldn't do much walking, because after a short time he's very out of breath and his chest hurts, so I suggested we have a drink and just chat inside on his comfy sofas. He was up for it. We had a long talk, a mixture of subjects, but one fascinated me. How he sees woman now versus before. He so loved my mum with all his heart and would do most things for her but before her, he was quite the ladies man. He was a wonderful caring man. In my eyes he was always very patient with my mum and he completely respected her. She couldn't of had a bigger cheerleader. Now saying that they had their clashes, but what marriage doesn't? They were together for 30 years. How many marriages last that long now? This is because they truly loved each other. My dad was a very good looking man, even as he got older, so he was very popular with the ladies, but I'm so thankful he met my mum, which made him be my dad.

It came to that time where dad was tired again, so he went up to sleep. This happened so many times in the day. When I planned coming over I really didn't expect that and hoped to do more with him. I decided to go outside into my old back garden. It was the same…just a little less lively. All the bushes were there, even the massive tree in the middle of the green acting like a big umbrella for that patch of grass to shield from the hot Santa Clarita sun. The Jacuzzi was sitting there looking dull like it hadn't been used in years. The sun beat down on me and I took in the heat that my soul misses. I got the camera out, and as a crazy tourist in my own home town, I made some footage of the beautiful weather heating up my garden.

I decided to try one of dad's favourite pods and by golly that's a roast and a half. That's a mummy roast, you know when you need something to really wake you and get you through the day, and when your child has got you up a million times in the night and every time he/she calls out 'mummy' your head kind of twitches like you think you can't cope…yes I've had many a day…we all have. Coffee, to my dad and I, is a much deeper experience than just having a hot drink in the morning. We have a connection with it that cannot be replaced with tea or diet coke or even caffeine pills. We have a true love for it. It's as if we have roots…or Columbian blood deep within. When I say I want it black….I'm not bragging, I just don't want any other flavours to disturb the beautiful natural flavours from bursting in each mouthful. Once in a while I'll have a cappuccino, but I'll have it dry (I don't get why it's called that because a coffee is always going to be wet) which means it's mostly foam instead of milk. I order this because I like the fun of the foam but much prefer a regular black dark roast.

Suddenly the time had crept up to when Paul was going to take me to his favourite burger place. I was so excited mainly because there has been so much hype about this place. We arrive, walk in and if I'm honest, it really doesn't look like much at all. We ask for a table and my brother looked shocked when the lady took us straight to a table. Apparently this place gets so pack you usually have to wait a long time to get a seat. We sat down and Paul handed me this meal form. You choose everything from the type of bun to what you want inside it, and then there is a space for you to name it. I obviously had to start with their namesake…the 50/50 patty. 50% beef and 50% ground bacon. It sounded like something out of a movie. I then added lettuce, tomatoes and avocado mash (to make it sound healthy with 3 of my 5 a day).

Then you get to choose your cheese, and there isn't just cheddar or burger cheese as I call it, you know those plastic looking yellow squares you get on burgers usually…oh no they had way more. I chose the homemade beer cheese.Then if that wasn't enough, you can then opt for more meat to go on top of all that! The greedy person inside of me then decided to add rosemary parmesan bacon strips on top with ranch dressing to finalise it. What a dream of a meal…or a heart attack. It arrived to the table in all its glory, and I honestly thought, this is everything and some of what I hoped it would look like. The bun was golden and glossy and nicely toasted on the inside. The salad items were fresh and crisp. The patty perfectly cooked and juicy, and the bacon strip was bursting with flavours. It wasn't any of that lifeless streaky bacon either, it was thick sliced meaty bacon strips. I took my first bite and I didn't stop till it was gone and I had taken my last bite. It was truly the best burger I had ever had in my whole life. How was I going to go home to a place that has burgers that don't even compared to the drive through burgers over here. I knew I wouldn't be able to go back again this trip but would I have to wait another 8 years? I had to find a way at home to recreate this beautiful burger.

If my inside had enough of fatty foods, they were about to be overflowing because Paul said we can't go to eat burgers here without stopping at this special donut/ice cream place down the road….after.

This place is an amazing pudding place where you basically choose what kind of donut you want and then you choose an ice-cream to fill it with. I honestly didn't have any room for this at all but Paul was not budging in any way. I chose an original glazed donut filled with a coffee ice-cream…amazing! I took one bite but you know when you get to that point where you either stop after that bite or you have another and you throw it all up…I was there. Paul's friend had to finish it and for some reason he looked like he could quite easily have had about 20 of them and not be full.We drove home and when we arrived back dad told us he had a bad nosebleed while we were out and it was still going strong. This made all the wonderful time with my brother change and gave me an overwhelming pang of guilt and worry and sadness. At any moment things can change with dad.

It was late and jet lag was still really difficult, but Paul gave me a little nudge of encouragement to go sit and talk with him. I walked into his room, and he was in bed with tissues stuffed up both nostrils and some sort of clip on top of his nose. It made his voice sound funny. I didn't tell him. We talked about the kids and what they loved at the moment and how he missed them and before long I couldn't keep my eyes open and had to say goodnight and go to bed. Dad looked sad I had to leave him. It broke my heart because I hadn't seen this vulnerable side to him since leaving home to move to England 8 years ago.

The day I had to go to the airport and leave my family to move to England was the first time I had properly seen my dad cry. Part of me actually wanted to throw the ticket away and stay because I hated the idea he was going to miss me that much, and I knew for sure I was going to miss him just as much. But I knew I had to leave my family home if I wanted to grow and get all the things I wanted in life. Sure it didn't have to be halfway around the world, but actually, it should have been expected. The thing is, in my family, all the women on my mums side have moved to a different country to be with their love of their life. So I hadn't met my love at the time of the move, but it was inevitable. Maybe that's why he was crying, because he knew I would meet someone and not come back. I had no clue of this at the time, and that's probably the reason I didn't rip up my ticket and stay longer.

As I walked to the bedroom, I thought of how many times I had walked these halls and gone to sleep in this house with my family. All the happy memories we had made. I had really missed all the carefree time I had here and all the love we shared as a family.

I remembered how many times my mum changed the look of my room to keep me excited enough to keep it tidy, and the time my dad walked down in just a towel because he didn't know my friends were over, and as the towel slipped a little, he revealed slightly more than my friends ever thought they might see of him.

All the beautiful wafts of food coming up the stairs or the freshly ground coffee smells making me run down to have grab a mug. It amazes me what things I can remember if I just stop and think and reminisce for a short time. Memories can stir so many different emotions in you, but the best ones give you a warmth inside that's better than a perfect temp hot water bottle can give you on a snowy night, and that, in itself, is what every human being needs to feel at least once in their lives

# Chapter 7: Friday...

I got up, got dressed and did the wonderful walk down the paseos towards granary square. I was meeting my friend April. This girl is an amazing woman to me. She is only true to a person and her heart is full of love that she freely hands out to everyone who needs it. She recently did the mother of all 'gifts'. She gave her mother-in-law one of her kidneys. She is selfless and has a beauty from the inside that also shines on the outside.

I used to work with her at a well know private school in our town in America. She was a teacher in one of the other rooms and I loved her from the first moment we met. Biggest smile around and always saw the good in everything. She's a silver linings kind of gal.

We had a lovely catch up, and it's true what they say, even if it's been years since you last saw each other (8 years in this case) true friends will meet up and it will feel like you haven't had any time in-between. It was cut short as Paul had planned a lunch with the family and I didn't want to miss that. Me, dad, Paul, my cousins and my uncle at this well known Italian chain restaurant. I used to love it when I lived here, but Paul had mentioned there was tasty lunch offer with some delicious soups I must try. Boy do I love a good deal.

Dad's always loved soups and I could see he was quite excited too. I'm not one of those types of people. If i'm eating soup, you know i'm on a diet or i've got the flu. Or it's 20% soup and 80% rice/pasta. Anyway, Paul kept banging on about this one soup with gnocchi in it and told me to order it because its unlimited...but that goes against everything I stand for with dinning out...so I ordered the salad with ranch dressing and pasta with alfredo sauce. Sure ordering a salad out is wrong but not this one, and it was perfectly paired with pasta so it worked. It didn't disappoint either, but also I got to try Paul's soup and to my shocking surprise it was just lovely. Lovely but not amazing enough to order it again. Dad finished his bowl of soup the quickest I had ever seen since I had been here, which was weird for me because most of the other food he would leave or take a long time to just eat a few mouthfuls. In fact he ordered a second bowl.

Years ago I remember him and my mum loving this one lentil soup that they would add coriander, avocado and a squeeze of lemon juice to it and he couldn't get enough of that either. It just looked like something my dog would eat, brown mush in a bowl, so I wasn't interested at all. That was the only thing he was interested in as far as health food was concerned

for many years. He had a very sweet tooth and he loved fresh bread and proper fish and chips. It wasn't till quite a bit after I had moved to England that he got interested in going to the gym and drinking freshly squeezed orange juice in the mornings. The thing with the cancer he got, none of the gym or healthy eating would spare him from getting it. In fact, dad was the fittest he had ever been when he actually was in contact with the asbestos. He didn't even see it. There was no way of him preventing it, yet it was a completely 100% preventable cancer. That's the saddest part of getting hit with this news. If he hadn't chosen to work on ships would he have been spared the awful time cancer has given him? I know for a fact dad would not have chosen a different life. He so enjoyed seeing different countries and this was the cheapest way to do that. Boy did he see a lot of the world this way. He made some great friends, in fact one friend, Chris, is known as his 'oldest friend' because he met him all those years ago and they are still great friends today. Not to forget this is also how he met my mum and if he hadn't met her I wouldn't not be around. No me, no Paul, no mum. Don't think he would have been as happy for so many years. But you can not think this way. It just eats away at you and makes you feel sad inside. Life is how it is because that is what we choose. And what a beautiful life he had. That's all that matters.
It came to the time to do skype with my family again and I really looked forward to talking to them and seeing their little faces. I've been away from my little boy now for a couple of days now, but it already seems like he knows new words or should I say the words he could say before he now says clearer. And this sort of thing makes my heart a little sad as i'm not there helping him with that. He's got all that from while i've been gone. He's done it without his mummy. My little girl seems taller in the last

couple of days, and for any of you that know my daughter, this is not possible. She is proportionate in every area but she is quite possibly the smallest little girl you will ever meet. She doesn't have tall parents so that was inevitable. I really look forward to giving them a big squeeze when I get back.

This evening my brother wanted to go to his favourite restaurant. He said it's the best place to have dim sum. I've never had dim sum so I have no comparison but Paul…he has had a lot. We drove to Pasadena and I started to get excited. On the freeway I just continually thought…I wish dad could be with us. I wish I could share this experience with him. To be fair, he would have hated it. The majority of the food was going to be pork. Dad hated Pork with a passion. He used to say he was allergic to it but through the years it gradually changed to him just hating it.

We parked the car and walked to the place. On the way we walked through this beautiful piazza with fairy lights and shops galore. Restaurants on every corner and amazing fountain shows shooting up and down in the sky like a water roller coaster. We walked into the restaurant and put our names down on the long list of hopeful diners. The wait was 45 minutes and not too bad considering time and day so says my brother. We decided to go for a walk. We didn't go far, because next door there was a place that sold lemonade which amazingly made different flavours of lemonade. The flat non fizzy kind. My favourite. Chris, Paul's friend ordered grapefruit flavoured lemonade. He let me try it and it was amazing. We then went into a couple of shops and then it was time to go back to the restaurant. As we walked in I looked around. It was a very nice restaurant but looked expensive. We were showed to our table and Paul instantly started telling us what we should order. I had to trust

him. We ordered and it came soon after. All fresh and piping hot. It all smelled amazing and visually made me want to keep on ordering. When we finished I had absolutely no room left in my tummy...and yet we headed towards the factory full of cheesecake...to pick up a to-go cheesecake of course!
We arrived back and dad had just got up. He was still a bit sleepy and headed straight to the sofa and put the tv on. I got a hot drink and sat next to him for a chat. Dad and I reminisced about all our Santa Barbara trips and how much he loved the zoo for the crooked necked giraffe (who has sadly passed away since the last time we went). We talked about how much the beach was a favourite place for us. How as soon as we step on to the sandy beach we feel a special kind of happy and we both feel calmer when we are near the sea. This must have been the reason why he chose to work on ships back in the day. I sipped my drink and felt like although my dad and I talk everyday, sometimes through texts and sometimes through a phone call, I really missed just this. Sitting next to him, face to face, having a chat. So simple, and yet so hard for me to do since living so far away from him. I remember the first time he came to England to visit me for my wedding. When he arrived and that first hug he gave me, I remember thinking the same thing. I just so wish I could be back and forth more often to see him.

# Chapter 8: Saturday…

On the day I was leaving, my brother said he would take me to the airport…this was big for him because if there is anything he does not like…it's taking someone to the airport. We decided to go to his friends coffee shop and get some coffee first and then head to a donut shop for a last indulgence. Unfortunately, it wasn't the best donut shop for me and they weren't hot, but they still were quite delicious, and paired with the strong hot coffee I was just happy. We got a few extras to drop off at the house for the housemates as an act of kindness and before long Paul said we had to leave. Before we left Santa Clarita we stopped for a slice of the cheesiest pizza you can get for $1.50. It was great all those years ago as it was today. If we hadn't have got the donut I would have got one of those large churros for $1 as well. Best priced food around. I would not need anymore food for the rest of the day!

As we got closer, he said we would stop at 'Little Tokyo' as it was very close to where we were going and he wanted me to taste the best kind of raumen around. I was sure I wouldn't have any room for that but I went along with the plans.

We got to the car park and parked the car. As we shut the door, Paul said to me,

"When we leave the car park up until we walk into Little Tokyo, walk fast and stay close to me"

I didn't know if this was one of his sick jokes, or if he was telling me what I needed to know. All I know is, I've never seen my brother as someone who can beat off strangers (although 8 years on and he definitely has muscles now) but in that moment, I was very aware of his 6'2 height…and big is big! So I walked fast and I stuck close. But as it happens, the minute we walked out, a man who acted as if he was the man who crosses the street shouting "Holly-wood…what's your name" in the movie 'Pretty Woman' started walking behind us. But he looked like a much scarier character, with all his clothes consisting of dark colours and a cap under the hood of his jumper to hide most facial features.

Once we got to the destination I instantly relaxed. It was beautiful. Lanterns hanging everywhere, floral decorations, smiley happy people. It was exciting and it felt like we had walked into another country. I walked into a shop selling lots of little trinkets. I found a thousand things I wanted to get but ended up leaving with a set of fancy chopsticks for my mum. She loves to eat Chinese food with these instead of forks and always asks for them at restaurants, so I thought getting her a special pair would be a sweet thing to bring home for her.

We continued walking and Paul said I had to try this traditional ice-cream they were selling there in cute little flat balls. It came in a flavoured rice flour pouch. There were many different flavours to choose from but I stuck with chocolate. I took a bite and as I swallowed the thick paste-like consistency, I decided that I was quite confident in saying, there was no chocolate in it. It was coloured in a soft brown chocolate colour, but the flavour had no excitement that chocolate gives you. At least I can say I have tried it now.

We heard music ahead of us and Paul said the guy who was making the music was actually pretty famous. We listen for a bit. The man was quite a jokester as well picking on people nearby but making them laugh in the end. We sat down and looked at the time, and it was time for this 'best' raumen. If i'm honest, I was in no way hungry as we had eaten a lot of really heavy foods already today. It was my last day in America and I was trying to get all my favourite foods in one day. What I had forgotten was, there's only a certain amount of room in my stomach to hold everything. But I knew it would be a long time till the next time I would be there to devour them. The saying is "Go big or go home"...I got big when I went home!

We walked in and this place is nothing amazing to look at. In fact, it's not very big either. We sat at the bar, because all the people were crammed in every possible seat, and as you can imagine, it was also very hot in there. I really hoped this was going to be amazing food because the surroundings weren't anything to write home about. We ordered, I ordered mine without the egg. Paul ordered some drink that was disguised as coffee but tasted like sugar syrup water. I stuck with water. As I sipped at it, I look around and a man was walking towards me with a massive bowl of something. I was praying it was not for me...it was for me. How was I going to eat this? It was bigger than my head and deeper than a pool. I was going to waste some of it. Most of it. There was no way I would even get through a third of it. I could hear my mom's voice in my head saying

“There are hungry kids in Africa who would love to have your food”

Paul said “Isn’t the broth amazing?”

I looked down at the bowl and in real life I would never have order this. It really did not look appealing at all. It reminded me of a bowl of dirty water with things floating in it. Something you would find in a sewer, not in a bowl you are about to eat from. Never in my life would I go to a restaurant and order this. But I knew my brother loved it and I wanted so badly to have one more great moment with him before flying back to a country where I never see him.

I took a spoonful of the broth. I felt like I was on one of those shows where the people have to eat whizzed up bugs to get the points to go further in the competition. I could feel myself gagging already before it even entered my lips. They say you eat with your eyes. I think I hid the disgust quite well. Then I put it in my mouth and swallowed. What happened next, nobody could have guessed.

“It’s really…yummy” and I meant it. Boy when they say ‘don’t judge a book by its cover’ it’s completely true in this case. I went for a piece of pork next. It was so tender. It came apart like butter. The bean sprouts gave an amazing crunch among the other textures in this one bowl. The noodles were soft but just meaty enough to beef up this dish. It was such a shame I had eaten all those other things in the morning because if I hadn’t, I would have had enough room to finish.  We paid the bill and headed to the car.

It was now time to go to the airport and say our goodbyes. I knew this would be hard and was dreading it because I had no idea when I would see him again. I knew I would cry, I just didn't want to be drowning in tears. I would miss him. I wondered if he felt the same.

I got to the airport and we said our very brief and slightly awkward goodbye and then I made my way through security and eventually on the plane trip home. I felt sad to leave not just because I was going to miss them, but because I really didn't know when I would be going back. I desperately wished I could stay till dad was better and cancer free, but chemo sessions alone would take us into January and then there was the surgery and finally radiation. Just being away for a week was a long time to be away from my kids and husband, and I knew that being away longer wasn't really a choice as the children were still quite young. If we lived in the same country it was definitely doable, but living a 12/13 hour flight away was a no chance situation.

I arrived home after many hours of travel and was given lots of love when I opened the door to my family. I could tell they had missed me. In the months since I came home, my dad has been having lots of dizzy spells and feeling really nauseous. I got messages saying he had fallen on the concrete just outside our house and a picture of his face full of blood. The doctors have advised him on having more water as he's not having enough. I know I don't have a right to judge, but if I knew something was going to help me save my life, I would just do it. Parents often say to their children, when they have to have medicine, "You have to have it so just take it please". Why is it when I say the same to my dad, pleading with him, it doesn't work? I try to compare what he is going through like the first stages of pregnancy. Big mistake. This was not very sympathetic of me but I wanted him to feel like if I got through that then he can get through this. But as soon as I said it I knew it was the completely wrong thing to say and I immediately regretted saying it. I mean what was I thinking saying that to someone who has cancer? Someone who not only had cancer but was also not coping very well with it. I just didn't want to lose my dad. Sometimes when the problem looks hopeless, solving it in your head is the worse thing to do but because your head and your heart are so completely confused, the very thing you had thought would help…doesn't.

It's always been hard to get dad to listen to the doctors. I'm convinced he probably felt bad for a while before actually going to the doctors. If I know him well, he probably left it till he couldn't cope with it anymore. This should be a lesson to anyone reading this. Don't leave it too long to go to the doctors.

It's better for them to say nothing is wrong you are all ok, then them come back to you and say you have cancer and its already between stage 2 and 3.

Anyway, my dad has promised me he would try harder to drink more, so I'm sitting in a different country, praying, literally, he sticks to his promise. I do hope he does sticks to his promise. It must be hard to like drinks when your taste buds have been really thoroughly changed by chemo. Having to keep drinking fluid so you don't dehydrate and eat food to give you energy and keep some weight on, whilst the whole time it tastes horrible no matter what you have been given. I pray I never have to go through that, because just like my dad, and probably most people, I would struggle with it.

# Part Two:

# Chapter 9: January 4th 2017 Wednesday…

I remember this day well. I woke up thinking "Yay! it's dads last chemo session!". I sent him a picture message saying 'last day of chemo' and that I was very proud of him. It was almost as if a big heavy brick had come off my shoulders. Dad had really struggled with each session and it was finally going to be over. Only two more things to get over then cancer free. Then he can start living again. Five and a half hours later I text him to ask if he had finished yet, and he said the doctor wanted to talk to him first and he was running an hour late. I was desperate for him to finish so I could talk to him and congratulate him for getting through it all and push him to be brave for the next stage…his operation. Then at 20:22pm I

received a message from my brother that broke my world.
"Bad news. The cancer has spread and chemo isn't working. Chemo and surgery cancelled. It's in the bone so stage 4"
So my poor dad had turned up excited, almost, at the idea that his chemo sessions were going to be finished after today, and in a sick twisted turn of events, the doctors have said no more chemo and the cancer has spread.
I immediately text everyone i knew who was romotely religious and asked them to pray for a miracle. As much as it sounded bad, miracles happen everyday, and i wanted my dad to be one of them.
Dad and I then text about how he felt the appointment went and he basically was either very positive or just in complete denial, because he said that they had not said 'it was terminal' and 'he only really had one lung damaged'. I didn't want to admit it and I didn't even say it to him. But I knew he was in trouble, even though he was almost convincing me. I needed to go see him again. I dreaded telling my family since I had only just been there in October. I wanted to be there now, but it wasn't that simple. How were we going to buy a ticket to America? With me not working we weren't rolling in money. But I just knew in my heart I needed to got over there. I needed to help him live. So again I talked to Matthew and then we looked at different dates to go over. The best time would be in February but that seemed a long time away. My home group got together and on one of the Thursdays presented me with a bunch of flowers and an envelope with some donations from everyone to help us buy my ticket. I actually cried. They love and care for me that much that they got together and made this sweet kind gesture. I feel so blessed to have them in my life. They really are my extended family.

The following Tuesday he had an appointment with his doctor, and this is when I started feeling dad giving up. Just little things here and there that he said to me. This is really when I noticed that he would not make a lot of sense at times too and at other times it was like I had my old dad back. I reminded him I was not ready to lose my dad and he needed to carrying on getting through this. His reply was,

"I'm not ready to go either, I still have a lot of living to be had"

I wanted to ask him what 'living' exactly he wanted to do, but he had to sleep again. My uncle text me the following week to say dad was going down fast after I had asked how he thought he was doing. Getting that text from my uncle meant only one thing. I needed to change the date of when I wanted to go and it needed to be for yesterday. The closest date I could realistically do was the weekend, as I would have to sort out childcare now. I got my bag out and started stuffing some tops and a set of pj's. I had never packed like this. I hadn't made a list and it wasn't months before I was leaving. I would not have time to sit down and make a list. I was leaving in a couple of days and I had so many other things to do, normal everyday life things that had to be up to date before I left. I needed to plan to do the things I should have done with dad in October. I started researching the cheapest wheelchair and I arranged for friends to take us to Santa Barbara one of the days. Another friend bought me a ticket to Disneyland to help the cost. I got a complete stranger from a foodies facebook page to make me a fruit Christmas cake so we could have one last Christmas. I packed Christmas napkins, Yorkshire pudding mix and a Christmas card. I arranged people to drive me places because I knew my brother wouldn't be able to leave dad alone for very long. My brother kept saying to me he was sure I wouldn't be able to do these things with dad but I was so sure I would make these things happen. I wanted these memories more than anything.

As it got closer I knew I was in not a good way to fly as I had got what could probably be a chest infection. I say this because I didn't have an actual diagnosis as I didn't want the doctors to say I couldn't fly. And to add to this horrible sickness my left rib was very painful. To say I was worried was an understatement. Part of me worried I had the same cancer my dad had. It felt like it was getting worse with every cough. I took painkillers and throat lozenges but nothing really worked. On top of that, I had the awful guilt for even complaining about feeling unwell when my poor dad was possibly dying.

On the 21st of January, thinking I might lose my dad, I text him

"Dad can you please give me your recipe for that seeded bread you used to make?"

His only reply was

"Later".

# Chapter 10: January 28th Saturday…

Today I went to pick up Marlia from preschool and as I got closer to where she was sitting, I didn't see a dad kneeling down with his legs out among the crowd. I tripped hard and fell to the ground. I heard my rib click but worse than that…it was so embarrassing. I was on the floor of my daughter's preschool.

My glasses were all steamed up and people crowded around, including my mum who acted like I was dying. The dad felt so bad, you could just tell in his face and he was so apologetic that I actually felt bad for him. I got up and was fine but in a little extra pain. Marlia was a little worried about me too which was really sweet but also made leaving the preschool twice as long, with all the "mummy are you ok?".

For the next couple of days I prepared dinners and washed clothes and put them in piles to help my Mum and Matthew, and as quickly as that, the day came that I was leaving again. Marlia was sad, I could just tell, but she was being brave and telling me she would see me soon. Milo was crying his little heart out and he was definitely going to miss me. Although Matthew was choked he pulled himself together. We were both going to miss each other. We knew how it felt to not see each other for a week since we had to do it not that long ago. It was still a very vivid feeling of missing that already began as we stopped holding each other and said our goodbyes.

I got into the car and waved as we turned the corner. I felt sad for so many reasons. Sad for my family missing me, sad for me missing them and sad for the journey I was having to take. I just wish I had magic pixie dust to sprinkle over this whole situation to make it all change for the better. We got there in record time and instead of delaying my walk in, I decided to just go in and get on with it. I said goodbye to Corina and Alex and they both hugged me as if to say they were there for me if I needed them. They waved goodbye and I walked into the airport.

This time I thought I would go straight to get something healthy to eat as I knew from this day forward I probably wouldn't be taking smart choices as far as food goes. I am mostly definitely an emotional eater, and I knew for sure there were emotional days ahead. Funny enough, everything I chose made me look like a proper vegan, (so many of my friends are vegan now and I've always said it would be too hard for me) and so I quickly picked up one of those chicken on a stick packs. I have nothing against vegans, I just think in my head, not having meat would mean soon i'd be hungry again and I didn't want to then go crazy on crisps.

Before long it was time to board the plane and find my seat. This trip I was going to watch lots of movies and hope for the 12 hours to literally 'fly' by. This flight I'm sat next to a woman who tells me she hasn't been working for her company for very long and they are already sending her and her team out to Los Angeles for a week. I congratulate her and then almost instantly the dreaded question comes out.

"Why are you heading to LA? Business or pleasure?"

I could have just said holiday, or going to see family, but the first thing that came out of my mouth was,

"I'm coming to see my dad before he dies"

Well this girl clearly wasn't expecting that because her response was a big loud half laugh half cough. She obviously had to follow it up with a quick…

"I'm so sorry, I hope it goes ok"

Although I was quite poised when answering the girl, when she replied, I felt all the emotions boil up inside of me and to try to stop myself from crying, I put my headphones on and searched happy children's songs and literally listened to the whole album, of a well known American explorer children's cartoon who teaches you Spanish whilst on her adventures. Basically it was because it didn't remind me of my dad in any way. After I had listened to a dozen songs and felt like I was back in preschool, I was fine.

But it was definitely a bit weird for the next 12 hours, especially around drinks and dinner time. She felt obligated to offer her free alcoholic beverage and any of the sweet stuff we had for pudding, to I guess cheer me up. It was going to be a long flight.

We finally arrived and I hurried through to get my bags and get to a telephone. I called Josh, Christina's brother, and told him I had arrived and he said he wouldn't be long but to look out for him. Josh arrived and I climbed into his big truck, actually I think I jumped in to be more accurate. It's always nice to see someone you count as family. Although he's younger than me, I've always thought of him as my older brother. He is of course not my actual brother. We are not even 'real' family but him and his family have always felt like my second family. I spent most of my free time in their house and stayed there whenever I could. It was the best place to go.

Josh's sister, Christina, is my best friend and we had so much fun together. She was the sister I never had but wanted. I had really hoped I would have seen her on either of these two trips but she lives in Seattle and is a teacher so it hasn't been possible. Hopefully soon one day we can see each other and introduce our children to each other, because without her in my life I'm not sure where I would be.

He drives me all the way to Susan's house, which is the opposite way to his home, in fact his house is 5 minutes away from the airport so he's really going out of his way for me, and with no expectation of payment but I give him some English chocolate. It doesn't quite feel enough for all him and his family have done for my family, but I give it to him anyway. Susan opens the door and all I can think about is I can finally stop and go to bed Up early tomorrow morning to go get dad some smoothie ingredients and fill him with good nutrients. That would make him feel much better. I knew it wouldn't cure him but it might make him live a few months longer and his last months a bit better. I got into to bed and before long it was 2:30am and I was wide awake. This is what jetlag does to me, but the one thing I love about Susan, is that she wakes up everyday at 5am. So that's means from 5 I have human conversations. If I stayed with my brother nobody is up until 9am. That's a long time to be sitting waiting for life to begin.

# Chapter 11: Sunday…

So Susan and I enjoy coffee together in the morning. We chat and discuss what's happening with dad and because she is such a lovely caring woman she tells me she is around for me this whole week for driving me places. I don't know what I would have done without her. She has really been the solid ground I have needed through all this mess. We get dressed and head out to the supermarket as early as possible. I was eager to get all the best food, and once I've bought practically all their fresh fruit and vegetables and ziplock bags to make individual smoothies, she drops me off to dad's house. Paul answers the door and asks me what I have. He kind of looks at me as if I'm a crazy person. I tell him I know dad can't eat but I'm going to make him healthy smoothies and he can drink the goodness into him. But in the middle of me saying this, he interrupts me.

"Ang…dad can't really drink…he stopped eating and drinking on Wednesday"

My heart felt like it had stopped. Everything in the room was spinning and I felt a horrible pain in my chest. I was too late. How did I not know this? The doctors said he had about a year to live a couple of weeks ago. I was going to help him live just a little bit longer, but actually now I knew, I was just here to see him till he died. I can't even tell you how devastated I was. My dad was going to probably die this week, no he was definitely going to die this week and there was nothing I could do to help him. I felt like I was going to throw up my emotion.

"Come on, let's go upstairs and see dad"

I felt scared of being able to hold in my emotions and I didn't want him to see my reaction to having to say goodbye. I walked into his room. I saw him lying on his bed. It was dad, but it didn't look like dad. It looked like the cancer had eaten him. He looked more than anorexic. He was just literally what people sometimes say but don't actually mean…'skin and bones'.  He was in a lot of pain. I was scared to see him like this. I mean what the heck happened? I had only just seen him in October and now it was January and the difference was immense. My head hurt and I couldn't think straight. Paul said we needed to bed bath him. This upset me. Not the fact that we would have to clean him, but the fact that this amazing man, my hero, had got to such an awful point that he was having to depend on us to clean him. Cancer had taken my dad. I was so angry…but also so completely shocked.

I feel ashamed really, but when I saw my dad, I felt scared to touch him or even get close to him. I tried not to show this feeling to my brother because I didn't want to upset him anymore than he already was and I wanted him to think his older sister could deal with stuff like this. Hard hitting painful imagery that hurts you in places you didn't know could hurt. He already looked like death had got him. He didn't look like my dad. I heard my brother say

"Just talk to him, hug him"

I was in way too much shock to do either but I said deep in my heart, god give me the strength to do this please. I slowly made my way to his bed where he lay there in pain.

"Hi dad, I'm here" I said all choked up inside. All he could manage was a very small "hi" in a dry voice. His room was filled with stuff. My whole life his room has always been like this. He hoards things, specially paperwork, books, stationery and computer things. His whole world was in this room. A whole bookshelf of astrology books. Drawers among drawers of gadgets and electrical things. I know this is where I get it from, although I'm definitely not as bad, I am sure my husband and friends would say otherwise, but they wouldn't if they saw what I had seen. We both love journals and new pens and can't go into a stationary shop without coming out with something new.

I look back at dad and he reminds me of this one day last week when I walked past a hedgehog that had been run over. The weird thing was that it wasn't in the road it was on the pavement. Had a bike gone over it? No it had to be big fat wheels. It still had its trademark spikes and it still was the same colour a hedgehog usually is...but in a way something had been taken away from him, making him look less like him. Life had been taken away.

This is what happened to my dad. You could tell it was him, but all the life had been squeezed out of him.This completely crushed me. For the whole of my life dad had always been chunky legged, tubby tummy, big hands with chunky sausage fingers, and I loved him like this. He always gave me a big squeezy hug and I looked at him as a big softy. The man that was in front of me now was so far from that. My heart broke. He lay in bed in pain and weak. What had cancer done to him? There was nothing I could do for him now but be with him. I knew at this exact point he was going to die this week. I've never been in this position before. I didn't ever want to be here again.

For the rest of that day Paul and I went through loads of dads stuff and got rid of some of it. It almost felt like he was gone already. Having to think "will we need this when he's gone?" and "do I want this as a memory of him to take home with me?". This was purely to make room for the hospital bed that was coming today. This would be much better for him because then he wouldn't fall out of bed anymore and he'd be a lot more comfortable as far as the bed being able to sit up easier.

There was a nurse coming for him today as well to hopefully up his pain meds to help him be more comfortable. This is something we really wanted because there is nothing worse than hearing someone you love make moaning noises because of the pain he was going through. And my dad had a strong pain threshold so I knew it had to be bad. Paul said it was time for dad to have one of his pills but as soon as he put it in his mouth it got stuck under his tongue. His mouth was so dry because he had stopped drinking days ago, he couldn't even take a pill anymore. Paul tried a couple of times to take it out but couldn't. Dad was frustrated and just wanted it out. Then I tried several attempts and it wasn't till I think the six or seventh time I finally got it out. It was very stressful and I know for me, I just didn't want to hurt him any more than he already was. We gave him a sip of water but he just choked on it, so we just gave him ice chips from then on in. He seemed to be better at chewing that.

The day just seemed to get worse as dad was so fed up by then, he actually shouted “I want to die”. I literally prayed those wouldn’t be my dad’s last words to me. I asked for dad to be taken out of pain as soon as possible so he could be calmer and not agitated anymore.

A lady from hospice care came over and gave us a folder to give us all the information we needed to know about when a person is about to die. I thought this was so strange. It actually gave you a step by step guide of what to look out for, and what to say to your loved one, when you know it’s coming close. This concept of knowing when someone was going to die really shocked me. I had always felt like with death you have no clue, but this folder told us dad was going in the next day or 2. That afternoon the nurse came and told us to give dad Morphine every 2 hours and some other drug the opposite 2 hours so he would be getting medicine every hour. He also said dad had a fever so we had to give him medicine for that to every 4 hours. This was a little scary for me since we were not nurses and these medicines were not like the fever medicines I give my kids. These were hardcore meds to conquer really tough pain to the core.

We walked out to the hallway and the nurse said that we might be getting another nurse for the night tomorrow to help us, and you could just feel the relief from both me and Paul. In truth, dad should have had that a while ago, but the hospice care in America is shocking compared to England if you don’t have lots of money. That’s not saying the care the nurses gave him was shocking, because they were brilliant, it’s more about what you’re entitled to over there versus over here.

I asked the nurse how long he thought we might have with dad, and he said "tops 3 days, but I don't think it will be that much". I knew he was right because even me, a non medical professional, thought it would be tomorrow.

The folder had said that sometimes your loved ones just need to hear you say "It's ok, you can go now, we will be fine" and then they are ready to pass away. So Paul and I both agreed we needed to say that to dad. We went into his room individually to have this chat with him. I was dreading it, mainly because I was going to have to tell him something I really didn't believe. I wasn't going to be fine and I'm not ready for him to go. But I also knew he would be better off in heaven. So I told him

"Dad, It's ok, you can go be with your mum and dad now. I'll be ok. I love you so much" It literally almost killed me to voice these words, but thankfully I did, because he replied with

"I love you ange".

# Chapter 12: Monday…

Today I woke up unlike any other morning I have ever had. Life seemed dark and horrible and I definitely didn't want to face the day. I couldn't sleep but I wanted to hide under the cover and come out again when everything was better again. I really felt drained from emotions from yesterday and felt like life couldn't get worse. I was so far from my husband who I just wanted to hold me tight and tell me things would get better. It literally took every bit of me to pull myself out of bed and go face the day. And this was all before seeing my dying dad. How was I going to cope with that? After a couple of coffees, to soften the blow, we made our way early back to Paul's house. As we pulled up, my heart started beating really fast and it felt like it was going to come up out of my mouth. I was so nervous and scared.

Susan gave me a sturdy hug as to say "I'm here for you, be brave", and I walked up to the front door. Even the knock on the door seemed harsh to me. Mihwa opened the door and as soon as I stepped in, I could feel all the emotions build up inside of me ready to explode at any moment. We walked upstairs and into dads room. There dad was. He looked the same as yesterday if not worse. I waved to him. He couldn't talk either so he nodded as a reply. I understood even though this told me he was near the end, because my dad always had words even at really bad sickness times, he would still tell me stories about how he didn't like a certain prime minister or why he loved pasties more than a sandwich for lunch. And boy would he have gone into detail as well. No...all words had stopped. I would never have to sit through a long dad story ever again...and yet I desperately, for the first time in our life together, wanted to hear one right now. Oh how I felt the guilt creep up inside forever complaining about them in the past. Guilt is such an awful feeling to be felt.

Susan stopped by to bring Paul and me some food. For the first time in probably my whole life, I did not want to eat. It just felt wrong to eat. I took the food and put it away and hoped later I would eat some.

As I was saying goodbye to Susan, a jeep pulls up outside the house. The lady came out and looked a little bit confused possibly because she had her phone on loudspeaker and was looking at a piece of paper probably trying to find our address. I told Susan this was probably the nurse that was coming over to see us and that I would have to go.

As I walk over to her, I can tell she is a very jolly person and seems like she has no clue as to what she is going to see when she gets in.

The first thing she said to me was

"Hi, (in a chirpy hi voice) I'm *Lara* (* this name has been changed) and i'm going to make you happy today"

I didn't want to be rude, but my dad was dying...how was she going to make me happy? She seemed a little too happy, and if i'm honest I kind of thought she must have been on happy pills. I thought lets bring her in to see what she can do for dad, then ship her out quickly because I didn't want anything to upset anyone.

She came in and do you know what, I don't know how she did it, but she actually made us laugh. She cared for dad like he was her own dad. I was in complete shock that someone could actually be like this, working with people who are dying everyday. She told us a story about her going on a trip somewhere and that she saw a sheep and then began talking like a sheep, because in her story the sheep were talking. I have no idea why she went on this trip, where she went or why there were talking sheep in it. All I know is that the way she was telling this tall tale, it made us forget for a few minutes that we were losing our dad. It made us feel normal, as weird as that sounds, but we could breath and not cry and could talk. And I completely thank her from the bottom of my heart for that. She wasn't silly the whole time.

Part of the time she was completely serious with us but in a kind and loving way. Telling us the signs he was close to dying, what kind of breathing he would have and what his oxygen level would be. It was good to know, because this told me he was leaving us this night.This was all kinds of sad for me, but as awful as this sounds, it was also a bit of relief. Once he passed, I wouldn't have to see him in pain again. I wouldn't have to have the sadness of not being able to do anything. And I wouldn't have to endure this most horrible time that was had by my family and I.

I stayed as late as I could before Susan came to pick me up at 9:30 and then I went back with her. Now at this point I'm pretty sure people must have been thinking why did I not stay. I really did not want to see the last breath my dad took. I was finding it so difficult to see him the way he was as is, and could barely keep it together around Paul to help him, this I'm sure would have topped me over the edge. I knew that the nurse would look after him and I would be there within 20 minutes of being called maybe even quicker. I laid down in bed, full of cramps from getting my third period in a month, and the second just three days after the last, and just thought about my dad. I kept thinking I hope he knew I loved him and I hoped he knew just how much I cared for him. After hours of questioning life and trying to calm my sadness, I drifted off to sleep. I literally cried myself to sleep. This wasn't the first time and I knew it wouldn't be the last.

# Chapter 13: Tuesday…

It was 2:30 in the morning, and something woke me. As I sat up I felt funny. I felt like I had just had a normal chat with my dad and things were ok…but instantly I remembered they weren't and threw that feeling away as just a nice dream that could never be now. I thought to myself 'had my dad died?'. I checked my phone but Paul had not called me. I shook the feeling off but couldn't quite fall back to sleep. I closed my eyes but was half awake with my phone as close as possible, as I felt I would be getting a call soon even if it didn't happen then.

At 4:33 I got that phone call, and although 8 hours before I had been praying for dad to go soon, to get him out of this pain, hearing the news crushed my very soul. My dad was gone. No more chats. No more cuddles. No more father daughter dates to Santa Barbara. I was fatherless.

I instantly cried my heart out. I went into the bathroom and called Matthew. I don't know why I called him in there instead of the bedroom that I was in, but I guess I felt rushed to get straight over and so thought I should probably get ready at the same time. I didn't know how I was going to say it through all the tears. He had said he would tell mum to make it easier. I was going to have to wake Susan up and get her to drive me to Paul's. I was nervous to wake her at this crazy hour but I needed to get there quickly. I called out to her and she got up and dressed in minutes, as did I.

I got there in 15 minutes and felt sick at the thought of walking into the house. Mihwa let me in and we went upstairs together. Even my footsteps on each step felt in slow motion but as if they were made of lead. I felt the dread lay across my body in a heap of heavy weight holding me down. I walked over to dad to give him a hug goodbye. I did this even though it completely freaked me out. I bent down and put my arms around him. He was so still and stiff and so far from what my dad looked like, that instead of comforting me, it freaked me out even more. I hugged him because I didn't want to regret it like so many other things I should have done with my dad. Regret hurts so bad and can really fester in you. It's not like any other feeling. All the other feelings, even the bad ones like grief, you can work through them and figure out a way to live with them. Regret is a feeling that you just need to throw away if you want to get through life. When things like this happen, life to you, just stops. And it is then that all the questions flood in. Why my dad? Why now? Why cancer? You suddenly don't know how to carry on with life. For me it took me a couple of hours just sitting drinking coffee with my brother before I could move. It almost felt like, what do I do now? I continually asked myself those questions. I still don't have the answers, but i'm breathing and walking and looking after my kids, and if I can just continue to at least do that, in time, hopefully I will be able to do more.

My Uncle came over and looked like we all felt. He said he woke up weirdly at 2:30 and felt like it had happened. My brother and I looked at each other and then explained about what time I woke up and how I had felt. The men who were coming to collect dad and take him away (even saying that sounds awful to me) arrived and went upstairs to do all that they have to do. I definitely did not want to be upstairs when they did that. That would somehow highlight he wasn't just my dad lying in a bed, but he was my dad…that was dead.

My brothers friend came over and was telling stories about dad and for a minute there I laughed. And it instantly felt awful. Guilt set in again. I shouldn't be laughing when my dad just died. What was I doing? My chest felt tight again and I went off into the kitchen and made more drinks. Well you know what they say about depression and not eating. I didn't care about food those first few days after he passed. I lived mainly on coffee and the odd thing here and there. But as soon as I got home, it was as if bad food was comforting me. I ate whatever I wanted. I felt less sad when I didn't have to worry about how fattening something was or how many calories were in it. But deep down I was very sad and I did not like myself. I sat down again and a memory popped into my head. I'm in the kitchen, and i'm about to make some bacon for me and my brother as a treat for him. He's always love the stuff and I wanted to do something to cheer him up. I go looking through the cupboards for a frying pan and I stumble across some really nice non stick ones still closed in plastic. I pull them out and am about to take the plastic off when dad stops me.

"I'd rather you didn't use them please. They are new and the other ones still work and I'd rather not have bacon cooked on them"

Dad has always said to us he is allergic to pork and he hates bacon. I'm 95% sure he's not allergic but I decide they are his pans and go with the old ones instead.

That was back in October. Fast forward to now, 3 months ahead, dad has died and I'm in the kitchen again, this time looking for a pan to fry sausages in, to make toad in the hole for my brother, because it's one of his favourites. I open that same cupboard. Those frying pans are still there, and they still have the plastic on them. Just three months ago dad thought he had years to use them, and now they are just sitting there still not being use. This made me sad for him. I couldn't bring myself to open them up and use them. It almost felt disrespectful as silly as that sounds.

I could hear the guys walking downstairs with dad. I moved my head so I wouldn't see him. Was this the lowest I would feel now? One of the men came back in to give us some information. Before he was done, he turned round and said to us

"Steve should be available to talk to you tomorrow if you want to" Paul and I looked at each other confused.

Dad was dead, and he was going to get cremated…how were we going to talk to him now?

Paul looked at the man and said "Steve?"

It turns out the man who runs the crematorium was called Steve too unfortunately. It wasn't this guys fault, and actually it was a bit funny in the end.

People sent messages all day to Paul and me to see how dad was doing, and it felt like all we kept doing was repeating a sentence that we really did not want to. So finally I said, perhaps the best way to get the message to almost everyone is to announce it on social media so that it's over in one big message. He agreed.

"**The world lost a great man today. He was the best dad a daughter or son could possibly ask for. He was also a wonderful grandpa to my kids who loved him so much. We miss him so much and it hurts so hard, but we both believe he is in a better place, not in pain. We love you dad so much, rest among the stars** x"

Susan came by again and brought more food. She so looked after me. I came outside to her and told her how I was doing and how I just couldn't believe I was here in my families home, and he was just not here. She hugged me tight, like a mother would do and gave me some words of wisdom. I am so glad I have wonderful people surrounding me in both countries. That was so comforting for me and definitely got me through those first months.

I got a message from Nancy asking me if I wanted to have a coffee with her. It was the best idea because I really did not want to be in the house for a while. I wanted to be away from where everything had happened. She took me to a coffee house in granary square. We ordered our drinks and went to sit down. About 2 minutes into our chat of what had happened, Sonny and Cher- I got you babe came on.

Anybody who is anybody knows this is definitely not the kind of music that plays in this type of coffee shop. It's in fact the complete opposite. It happens to be the most iconic song to highlight my dad to me. We used to sing it so loud together on any of our father and daughter days out. It

completely freaked me out and I stood up and demanded that we leave straight away in tears.
I'm completely sure that I could have left in a much calmer way, but sometimes situations make you react in really different ways. I'm know Nancy understood, you see it hadn't been long since she had lost her own dad. She knew the sort of grief I was going through.

# Chapter 14: Wednesday-Friday...

From 8am-8:30pm I went to the house to go through dad's things, Wednesday, Thursday and Friday. He had accumulated so many things in his epic life that now that he was gone, we all had to chip in and help get rid of the majority of things. I don't know what it is about memories, but you can find them in anything. My dad and I went to a 'paint your own' place once and dad decided to decorate a mug. I chose a plate. He used a bright red paint for almost all the mug including the handle apart from one small half circle part at the top edge. He then decided to paint a very small rainbow in that half circle space. It was the best mug. In fact I remember thinking, why didn't I do that? And it's so amazing, why can't I do anything that great? But it had always been like that. He was way more creative than I was, and I always looked up to him because of that.

We were going through his computer space and there sitting next to the monitor was that mug. That whole experience, the fun we had all came flooding back. It was a wonderful memory of just one of the father daughter days we had, but it also brought huge pain as I knew there would be no more. I saw his massive bookshelf filled with endless astronomy books and books about anything to do with stars (as in the ones in the sky) or astronomers. What were we going to do with all those books?

There were boxes and boxes of paperwork. I remember when I was living there, dads office always had so much paperwork everywhere. I think this is where I get it from. I opened up a drawer just to change it up a bit. I thought I'd won the lottery. A whole drawer full of pens. Coloured pens, biros, markers. I have a bit of a thing for this type of stuff. Another thing I get from my dad.

I took a break and Paul and I decided we needed to do a sort of memorial service while I was still in the country as dad would not be cremated for a while. So we started to invite people and was lucky enough to have a service provided for us on the Saturday. We didn't have long to get things ready, but if we started now, we could just get it done. We would still have to keep sifting through his things so Paul wouldn't have too much to do when I left, so we went back to the piles every now and then.

We had to organise pictures for a memory board, make memory cards of dad for people to take, and organise the actual service with the help of the pastor. I had to write something out that I would say as Paul said it would be too hard for him. I understood that feeling but also didn't know how I was going to get through it myself.

As the days went by, the things disappeared but there still seemed to be a lot left for Paul to deal with. I wished I could stay even longer to help him more. I wished there was a button I could press and it would deal with everything for us. Life's not like that. I was, in the end, happy I had gone through a lot of his stuff, because it meant I got to not only see the things that brought up great memories, but it showed me another side to my dad I didn't know. There was a bag full of dental things, toothbrushes, miniature toothpastes, even these travel toothbrushes that you don't need toothpaste or water with them. I had no idea he was so into teeth. The funny thing is, if you were to see all these things, you would expect him to have the most amazing set of teeth. I love my dad in the biggest way, but in all my years that I have been alive, he has never had amazing teeth. So why the massive interest? This is something I might never know, but will probably try to answer.

I also found a lot of pairs of brand new shoes, just sitting in a box in the garage. Shoes that not all of them were really the kind of shoes dad would have worn. I found a pair of shiny moccasins and instantly thought perhaps my dad had bought them one day to impress my grandma, my mum's mum. She had a thing for that type of shoe, especially if they were clean and shiny. She always said that those shoes are only worn by true gentlemen. She believed this so much she used this method to pick her doctor! As the story goes, she went to the doctors office and waited to see all 3 doctors come out as she filled in the paperwork before she added which doctor she hoped for. The first doctor came out with trainers, loosely tied and scruffy. She said no to him. The second came out with lace up shoes that were dirty. She said no to him. Then Dr De La Flor came out and he was wearing shiny moccasins and she just knew he was the doctor for her. He is actually not only an amazing doctor but a wonderful human being, whom my dad truly respected. My dad and him soon became great friends and I truly believe because they are both 'true gentlemen'.

In all the mess, i suddenly stopped what I was doing, and remembered that I had packed very light this trip and had only brought the trainers I was wearing as my only pair of shoes and none of my tops were black. What was I going to wear to the service? I had no idea about sizes over here or if I could really afford to buy anything. I called Nancy and asked for help. She is so lovely and to be honest I thought I had asked too much of Susan already. Nancy took me to two shops and it turns out I actually have really small feet. The first shop didn't have anything in my size (3 or sometimes a 4). And the second shop only had one pair in my size. It was the second shop where we got a top as well. I now felt it would be ok since I would have the correct clothing for the service. I thanked Nancy for all her help. It's when you have friends you can completely rely on, that's when you feel you can cope with almost anything. I will never forget all the help my friends gave me when i needed them the most. Some friends prayed, some friends gave me lifts, some friends brought food, some friends donated money to help with costs, some friends just listened, and some did all of the above. I'm so thankful for everything i was blessed with.

# Chapter 15: February 4th…

Today was the day of the service. Ironically it was also national 'World Cancer Day'. We had no clue when we booked it in, but it hit us like a ton of bricks. What a day to have a sort of funeral service for someone who died from cancer?

I got to Paul's early and it just seemed weird in the house. I had been there every day clearing things and yet it felt different. A different mood. Perhaps it was everyone anticipating the events that were happening today, or perhaps we had suddenly all just felt the loss, but either way, there was a sense of sadness in the house lurking over like a big black cloud. I so badly wanted to get an eraser out and take away all the black, but I knew this would take time, if all the advice everyone had been telling me was right, "You won't ever get over it, but you will learn how to live with it", people would tell me.

We collected all the things we needed to take with us and got into the car and headed out to the church. Again I felt nervous as I knew in not a very long time I would be standing up in front of lots of people talking about my dad, when I can't even mention his name now without pouring hundreds of tears out. We arrived at the place and we handed the things out to be displayed and gave the sound guy the music.

And then we waited to greet the guests. It's a very odd thing to do, welcoming people in to one of these services. You are completely devastated, and yet you really should greet people with a smile and a welcome. I found this especially hard since it had only been days since we lost dad.

Once the majority of people arrived we decided to start this service. The pastor did a little talk and then it was my turn to get up and say my piece. I could feel myself shaking everywhere and I could feel the tears and emotion build up inside. I just wanted to get through this without crying, but I knew that was impossible. I stood up and the walk from my seat to the stage seemed to take to take forever. I looked out to all our friends and then also thought about all the people who couldn't make it or we didn't get to invite because it was so short notice. I felt a bit like dad might have wanted more people to attend. I tried to blank that out.

I opened up my scrunched up piece of paper with my speech written on it and then read from my heart.

**"This is probably the hardest thing I have ever had to do, but I will try my hardest. Dad loved lots of things in life. He was very happy living in America with the warm weather. He appreciated the small things like wearing shorts almost all year round, when most people wouldn't.**

**Dad and I used to have days out together, mostly to Santa Barbara and visiting the zoo to see the crooked neck giraffe. We'd have fish and chips on the pier and get a coffee for the car ride home. No trip was complete without singing Sonny and Cher's 'I got you babe' the top of our voices on the way home.**

**He loved drinking strong coffee from his favourite mug and I think I inherited that love.**

**Dad should have been called inspector gadget because you couldn't walk into his office without swimming through hundreds of electrical things he had.**

**He loved rose flavoured Turkish delight, Indian curries and homemade bread. He probably got his love for these things from his other love...travel. He was fortunate to work on ships for many years and made lots of wonderful friends who some of them are here today.He was able to travel to Australia which is something he always wanted to do.Dad loved astrology. He was actually very well known for this. He made beautiful books with peoples birth charts in it. I know for a lot of his friends, looking up at stars will remind them of him.**

**He loved my mum so much, as she did for him, although they might not have lived in the same country, they never stopped loving each other.Paul and I couldn't have asked for a better dad and we will miss him dearly. Rest among the stars dad x "**

So glad that was over. I feel I said pretty much what I wanted to say and almost all of it without heavily crying to bits, well, i did, but at least i got through it. We then decided that Paul, me and his friends would go to the restaurant across the street for food with friends as a kind of 'wake'. It was actually nice and not sad. It was just a bunch of people, who loved my dad, eating together.

# Chapter 16: Sunday -Tuesday...

So when Paul and I decided to do a service while I was in the country, I had to change my ticket as I was supposed to leave on the Saturday. I really wanted to be there for the service but I knew that staying later would be hard for everyone back home. I asked everyone if it was ok, but deep down I felt very bad for asking again. It just felt like I was letting my family down because I hadn't planned anything for the extra days and they would have to do that without me. The airline was amazing. They dealt with it so quickly and were so kind. Just the way they spoke to me showed they actually cared that I had lost my dad and needed to stay. I couldn't believe how blessed I was. I know Matthew was worried for my health and my cough had got worse since I had been over. I knew that if I went to see a doctor, even with insurance it might still cost me money that we didn't have, so I just kept taking medicine that we could buy over the counter. I decided that for the next couple of days I would do my best to go through everything in the house. So for the next few days I would spend all day at the house going through things, shredding papers with personal details, checking if there was anything I wanted to take back with me to treasure as happy memories. I hardly saw the rest of the world. When we did go out to pick up food it was short, but it was good to not spend time seeing people who would stop and saying sorry for your loss because I would be constantly crying and once you have opened a portal, it floods out all day.

Paul and I went to say goodbye to my grandma and my uncle. I didn't really know at the time, but this probably was going to be the last time I saw my grandma. She was very sick with UTI's all the time and in the next couple of months they would be moving to Panama so they could afford more care for her. My uncle and her are still in Panama now, but I know it will be a long time before I'll be able to afford a trip over there, and if her health keeps getting worse, then the chances are we will lose her. The difference here though, is she has had a long and full life in comparison to my dad. It will still be sad, but it will make sense to me.

# Part Three…

# Chapter 17: February...

Eleven days after dad died and 4 days after I arrived back home, it was my mother-in-laws 60th birthday party. It was a big birthday that was to involve a big party and happy smiling people. This really was the last thing I wanted to do but I love her so much and I so wanted her to have a great day and she also deserved to have a really wonderful celebration because she is a beautiful soul who has been through alot.

So I went, along with 30 family members. At this point I was in a lot of pain in my heart and I couldn't see how it was ever going to get better. I didn't want to be around people. I just wanted to dig a hole, jump in and cover myself up. It felt like a jagged edge knife had cut a dad size hole out of my heart and the messy sharp edges kept touching each other making the pain recur moment after moment, deeper and deeper.

It was hard, but I got through it. I ate the food and smiled for all the photos. Eating was the only thing that was masking the pain. This was the start of my weight downfall. Unfortunately some people find that through depression or severe sadness, you don't want to eat or you are so overwhelmed with sadness you don't even realise you are not eating. For me it was very different. Food, and not diet or healthy food, was the only thing that got me through the day. It may not be the answer but I would say it was what got me through those first 4 or 5 months. It's just realising you can't do that forever and you need to get back on a healthy track eventually.

The first couple of months it's very hard to think of anything more than 'I need to breathe', for some, this might last longer than a couple of month but there will be a key moment where you will know you need to just get on with your life, you might not know how to get on, but there will be a key moment, you haven't stopped being in pain, but you have got to a point where you can add more thoughts to your head and you won't explode into tears everyday. This isn't to say you won't have a tearful day here and there, because you will. You might, like me, see a beautiful sunset, and instantly start crying because it reminds you of the one you love and lost. I have been told this doesn't go away, and I'm pretty sure that's true. For example, I walked into church the first time since coming home and dad passing. I knew it would be hard, but the moment I walked in I felt my chest start tightening and I felt the tears build up behind my eyes. I parked the buggy up to the table and took the children's coats off. As usual they both wanted the biscuits that is on offer as you come in at the coffee and tea table. I got them both one and then went up to get a drink for myself. I'm standing in line and an older member of my church comes

in being pushed in a wheelchair. He was walking on his own feet the week before I left to go see dad. He had been diagnosed with stage 4 cancer not that long ago, in fact it was around the same time as dad was told no more chemo and I guess he had got bad since I was gone. Suddenly everything felt too much, I felt suffocated and I just needed to get out. And if that wasn't bad enough, Liz walks in. Walking around, looking great even though she has just got over chemo and 2 surgeries. I now can't hold in the tears and I need to go out.
I don't wish Liz to have lost her life, not in any way, she is the most loveliest woman, but why did she get to live and my dad didn't? They got diagnosed around the same time but the outcome completely different. How can life give you something so horrible? I know there's a god and I know he is helping me through this but I would be lying if I didn't wonder why my dad had to go? I know he's way better off where he is now, out of pain, but why did my dad have to get cancer?
People say some really insensitive things when someone dies. 90% of the time it's not actually meant to be insensitive and comes from someone who is just trying to say something to make you feel better. I seem to have a lot more tolerance for older people, I'm not really sure why. Maybe because they come from a time where you didn't really show your feelings if you got upset, you just pulled yourself up and got on with the day. These days you are encouraged to open up and cry out your feelings no matter where you are.
In fact, it's a good thing I do because on the evening of the day dad died, an older lady of perhaps mid 60's early 70's said to me
"At least you had a good dad for all those years".
I nodded politely but deep down I wanted to shout back at her

"No that's not good enough, I should have had him till he was at least 80 not 68!".

Later on I found out she had grown up without a dad and it completely changed my view on that one comment.

The other set of people I tend to have a bit more patience for is people from church. I say that and it sounds like I don't go to church, but even after everything that has happened, I still believe in everything I believe. However I do find it hard when someone says to me,

"Just remember, you will see him again in heaven".

I understand that, but for me, that isn't a comfort at the moment. All it does is reminds me he is not here anymore and it's going to be a really long time before I see him again.

I guess the best someone can do is just give you a quick hug and then walk away. It's just enough to let the person know you are thinking of them. Someone said to me that because I loved him so much when he was alive, the hurt would kind of match because you loved him so much. This was the first nice comment, or should I say the first comment I could connect to since he passed. It was true, I did love him lots when he was alive. I still love him lots, that's never going to change. But somehow the comment validated that and I appreciated it.

A nurse friend of mine also said to me I shouldn't have had to do some of the things me and my brother had to do. We should have just been there to love him in his last days and not have to worry about anything else. This was also kind of a validation thing for me and I appreciated it as it made me so angry that my dad couldn't have the free hospice care he would have got here which would have meant Paul and I could have just loved him in the end.

Meanwhile, I’m also trying to keep it together for my mum. Yes my mum moved over here to be with me and her grandkids but she did think my dad would follow. The thing is, my dad, although born in England, he was more American than anything. Even some words he said came out a bit Californian and he was always going through a drive through instead of walking in. He was always going to live there, but I guess when you love someone, sometimes you don’t realize some truths. But she never stopped loving him and to this day is heartbroken to have lost him.

# Chapter 18: March…

March had come way too soon and Sam, my friend from church, had mentioned if I wanted to go back to America, at any point, I could fly with him on standby to make things cheaper. I really did want to go back to scatter dads ashes, so Matthew and I decided that this is what we would do, and I got packed quickly ready for that call at any moment.

It was baby Roberts birthday party today. I say 'baby' but he's actually 1. Robert is my friend Linda's son and for some reason, both my kids call him 'baby Robert' still. Anyway, you were there. Well not exactly. Your favourite wine was served on the table. Imagine that at a 1 year olds birthday. (It was clearly for the parents) To be fair I always look forward to this families parties. They always cater for adults and children and all the food and drink is top notch. It wasn't sad to see the wine. I imagined you had actually done that to make me smile.

Things like this happen from time to time, and as silly as it sounds, I would love to think it is you who keeps trying to remind me you are still with me. I don't care what other people think. All that matters is that I will love you forever and ever and I will treasure every moment I had with you.

So you remember that moment I talked about. That one that you know it's now or never to get my life back. That came two days before Matthews birthday on the 16th of March. I didn't magically get better that day after that moment, but I did start to think 'What can I do to help me?'.

I got my running trainers out, downloaded Map my run app and went out for a 'run'. Oh my days, twenty seconds in and I was panting, red as a tomato and I thought I was going to be sick. I also thought I had no idea how I was going to do this again. I so wanted to be great at it, and somehow make my dad proud, but this was really very hard for me, so i stopped and started a couple of times. I thought I would try with the food side of it instead. Cut out cake and giant piles of crisps and basically anything that didn't really help my body. This too was hard. I was deeply grieving whilst I was sleep deprived, sometimes because of my son waking up and sometimes because of just being sad, and there I was trying to take away the things that were giving me the will to keep going. My positivity level was so low which was foreign to me as I am usually a glass half full kind of person. I needed something to kick it back into place…and fast. Then it came to the last week of march, dad's birthday week. I so wanted to go on this specific date. I prayed and prayed that we would be called. Then on the 28th my phone rang. My heart pumped faster than I even remember it had ever done before. It was Sam calling. This was the first time Sam had ever called me, (we normally text each other) and I knew it was for only one reason. He had been called on standby. This was my chance to go back and scatter my dads ashes. To have a proper goodbye. To also have a chance to bring a part of him home with me.

I had to go but first I had a number of things to solve. Firstly, who was going to look after my kids? Mom was working, so was Matthew's mom, and Matthew.

I sent out a mass text to anyone and everyone…I just needed to go. I had to be there within 2 hours from when he called, and my house was about an hour and a half away.

The text message replies came in. None of the family could help. All at work or out for the day. Then I started on friends…at this point, Marlia and Milo had only been looked after by both nannies…so I was starting to come out of my comfort zone. Out of the ones who actually replied, they were too far away to get back on time.

It was time for desperate measures…I messaged Sarah from across the road. Sarah is very sweet and is a mum of two boys. I completely trust her but my kids hardly know her. But I was desperate to go.

I waited (not very patiently) for her reply. Thankfully I didn't need to wait as my mom called and said work had let her off early and she could look after the kids.

Now for quick transport. There was no way I could take the train now after all this time and taxi would be a lot of money…but taxi it needed to be. I called Matthew and without a blink of an eye he said use whatever money we have in the house to pay for it. What a husband. I think he must have known how important this was to me and just wanted me to have what I needed to get it done. I called the taxi firm and they said they would get here in 10 mins. I had 10 mins to get the last of my things together, say goodbye to my children and then rummage around the whole house to come up with the £70 I needed to get me to Heathrow.

The taxi arrived and the driver must have thought I was some kind of fruitcake. My head was so clouded by where I needed to be in the next hour and a half. There was a deadline and I was not going to miss it for anything. I could hear the clock tick in my head. I waved goodbye to my babies and felt deeply sad I didn't get to kiss my husband goodbye because he was still at work. It was so last minute, I thought I was prepared for this moment, but actually, I really wasn't. I was going to really miss everyone. But I was on my way and before long we were on the freeway.

My phone pinged to tell me Sam had messaged. It was not good news. There was something wrong with his train. Even though I was voicing "he'll make it, don't worry" my heart already knew I was not getting this flight, and i was crushed.

I had to keep reassuring myself that there was a reason for the trip to not go ahead. A later date was going to be better, even though it was the last thing I wanted. Sam had to go on another trip when he arrived and I went home on the train, feeling devastated that I would have to come home and tell my husband I had wasted £70 on a hope to go to scatter my dad's ashes. For a whole week and a lot of the next, I was really down about not going and it made me sad to do things again. I needed to find my way again.

We went back to waiting to go on standby with Sam again, but I just kept thinking, there must be a much easier way for me to get a cheap ticket over there. So I researched which months were the best times to go. The beginning of November was at a brilliant price, the cheapest I have ever seen a ticket to America. So it was just under 8 months away, but it meant I didn't have to be on edge or have a short trip of 2 days (which would most likely wreck me as far as sleeping goes since Milo still wakes me in the night several times).

I needed to buy the ticket before the price went up so after a quick brief chat with Matthew, we got it. All I needed to do now was raise the money to pay for dad's special scattering at sea which cost quite a bit of money. I knew I would find a way.

I thought about it for ages and came up with the idea of making prayer boxes. I had seen one on social media not so long ago and had always wanted one for me. I charged everyone £2.50 but I guess because of the nature of the reason why I was selling them, a lot of people were very generous. I was able to come up with my half of the cost. This was a great achievement for me. It made me feel like I had finally done something dad would have loved. I had felt so bad for not being able to go look after him when he was sick, apart from his last 3 days of life, that helping him now made me feel a bit better.

I wish I had been closer. I wish I had loads of money. I wish I could have taken his pain away and kept him alive. But life is not something you can control, as much as I keep trying, sometimes bad things will happen and it's how you survive afterwards that's truly what makes you. I keep starting and stopping as far as the running training went but I did do race for life for my dad in June. I truly believe even though i was stopping and starting again most weeks with trying to learn to run, it was keeping me afloat for all those months, and that's probably why I kept it going, but I knew I was not far from exploding. I was an actress, faking my happiness so nobody else would be upset, but a lot of the time I couldn't hold it in. Once the kids were in bed, I would breath and the tears would flood. I knew this wasn't right. I need help and was sick of waiting for a counselling session to come through for me. I tried getting counselling everywhere, but because my dad died in America and not in England, the only free counselling I could get was a waiting list of 8-12 weeks…it ended up being 30 weeks by the time I actually got a session.

# Chapter 19: September…

On the second of September I had my 35th birthday. It didn't feel like a day I wanted to celebrate. It wasn't because I wasn't going to get a present from my dad this year, because to be honest with you it's quite expensive to send packages to me and visa versa, so we didn't really do that when I moved over here, and I knew he would come see me instead at some point and to me that was much more valuable.

It was because it just reminded me so much that he was still alive on my last birthday. We made plans to spend my next birthday together, and now that would not happen.

I was completely spoilt, I always am but no matter what people did for me, I still felt that missing feeling. Still didn't feel like celebrating. The next

hurdle would be Christmas. That would be very difficult as it was the holiday that both my dad and I just loved so much.
The other hard thing was that september is when my daughter started big school for the first time. I had talked to dad about this very day and how i was worried she was going to be too small. Dad reminded me that she was completely ready for school and she may be small in size but she has a big personality. He was right. When i dropped her off, it was bittersweet because i wanted so desperately to call him and tell him about this experience, but instead i had to settle with talking to a picture.
This first week is when I was finally given a date for my first counselling session, and I did feel a little bit excited at the thought that finally I might get fixed and life could be lived again. But on the day that the woman was supposed to come see me, a minute before she was supposed to arrive she text me to say she had a puncture and couldn't make it till next week. This really upset me as I felt really let down and the thought of yet another week till I would get help really pained me.
The cloud on my head got darker. It came to the second week of the month and a good friend, Naomi Meyer Newland, of mine posted on her social media group, that she was looking for some people who needed to overcome grief/pains/fears to practise doing hypnotherapy counselling on. At this point I was ready to try anything because I was in a very deep dark cloud. I put the smiles on, mainly for the kids, but underneath it all, I really hated the world I was in. I couldn't see how I was going to be happy again. So I signed up for a session, and on the 18th I had my session with her.
It started with lots of questions, and not questions I was expecting. I thought she would ask me questions about my dads death and it would

be a dark space then filled with a bit of waving of a pendulum to knock me to sleep (you know the type that after you have gone down you suddenly start acting like a chicken). But actually, it wasn't like that at all. It was in her bright beautiful living room all comfy, and she asked me questions about me, and the future and when it came to the hypnotherapy, there was no sign of a pendulum, and I was fully aware of everything. It was a way of visualising something nice in my head, instead of the awful images of my last day with my dad.

I literally walked out of the session with my happy dance song in my head and felt a lot more positive about the future. I didn't forget that my dad had died and I still missed him very much, but the cloud wasn't as dark and I could see through it.

I was so thankful, and just wanted to cancel the other counselling session, but I thought, I've waited 30 weeks for this, I need to at least have a go. So on the 20th, the lady came to my house, and this time she actually arrived with no problems. She had smokers teeth and wrinkles I could live in. I still welcomed her in, even though I could feel instantly she was not a positive match for me or even a positive person in herself. We had a chat and I had to go through the whole story all over again and it didn't feel like how great I felt the other day with Naomi. It felt dark again. Some of the things she said to me in reply to what I had said about being very down, had actually instantly made me more angry at the situation and no longer positive. We finished the session, but I knew I would not be seeing her again.

Traditional counselling works for a lot of people, I'm not saying it doesn't, I just know it didn't work for me. People are naturally different so it makes sense that we all have different needs when it comes to working out grief

and how to live with it. I instantly booked in for one more session with Naomi to get me back to where I was just 2 days before, so I would be ok for the weekends events.
In the middle of July I decided to do something big in honour of my dad. I created an event on the seafront in my town where it would be a fun 5k run/walk to raise money for mesothelioma research. At the start it was just going to be me and a couple of friends just running and putting a fiver in each, but then somebody said to me if I was doing it on the seafront, then I would need to ask the council if it was ok, as another event might be going on at the same time.
So I asked the council and then it got a whole lot more complicated. If I was going to do it where I wanted to, I would need to do risk assessments and I would need to get insurance. So, I thought about it and thought, if I was going to do all this work then I should make it a proper event with lots of people. I charged people £3 to take part in the race which paid for the medals and the insurance and a few of the posters.
It came to the day and we had 30 participants of a mixture of friends and family and a few new people that I got to meet who actually lived in the same town as me, and lost their dad to mesothelioma as well. The town crier opened the race and I did a small speech and then it was ready to start the race. I couldn't believe how this whole event had just come together and ran smoothly. We as a group raised over £1,100 and a whole lot of awareness. It was amazing. I felt like I had done something to change the world and I had hoped I had made my dad proud. It made me eager to do it again next year, so I created an events page for 2018. This time my goal was to double the amount of participants and raise £2,000 for 'The Mavis Nye Foundation'. I'm sure I will do it but I would need to

start early and get it out on social media so lots of people would do the run. I got to work on creating the events page and waited for people to join from  all over the place. I suddenly felt like there was in fact a purpose for my life. I had to raise money and awareness of this cancer and get people to understand. Organising it has been a healthy way of turning my life around and I will always be very grateful and will continue organising this event for years to come.

# Chapter 20: November…

Well the months went by slowly. I was desperate to just get back over to America and scatter dad's ashes. I felt like I would probably get some sort of closure that I had expected from the service we did on 'World cancer day', but had come away disappointed that I just missed him more. I planned a few nice things and meetings with friends too, as I was desperate to have a good time in America since the last trip I had come away with a really sad vibe of the place. No fault of the country, just it's the place where dad died and everything I looked at from there brought sadness to me, when before it had only brought me joy.
The week before, I started all the usual tasks. Washed, folded and labelled all of the kid's clothes for the week. Put meals in the fridge and the freezer and wrote out a timetable that said what everybody was doing and at what time. Made sure the washing basket was very low (I don't

think I have ever got it empty) and made sure all the teachers knew when I was going to be away and when I was coming back.

I packed an amazing amount of chocolate to give to all my friends who had helped my family and I in our last year. I wanted to give back to all these people who I couldn't have got through it all without them. So why chocolate I hear you say? Well, chocolate is cheap and Americans love English chocolate, and what better way to give back than with something people love?

The day came and like the 2 other trips, we were all very emotional. Another lovely friend picked me up at took me to the airport. I got there again with hours to spare. I got through security quite quickly and as soon as I was on the plane, my nerves started to ease.

This time Susan picked me up from the airport. Again I had the trouble with my phone not working but this time I was able to find a payphone to call her.

Susan arrived with her lovely husband Dan and we then walked to the car to drive home. At this point, Susan's house was like a second home to me. I just hoped she wasn't getting fed up with me. Deep down I knew she wouldn't be, but it was always in the back of my mind because I never wanted to overstay my wolcome. My friends meant too much to me.

We got home and we all enjoyed a small glass of wine. I so enjoyed it and hoped it would help me sleep through the night, otherwise I would be waking up at the usual…between 2:30 and 4:30 and that wasn't good for anyone, least of all someone with the amount of things I had planned for tomorrow.

So then I woke up at 4:30 and got up and dressed to be ready to go meet the santa clarita runners at 7am. I was really nervous as I have never done a run with a group that I don't know, apart from races, but this felt different. My tummy churned and I almost said to Susan that we should maybe leave it for today. But then a little voice in my head reminded me that new things are good to do and how often would I be here anyway? We left the house and went to lowes carpark as the ad had said that was the meeting point. However when we got there, no one was waiting. Susan drove all over the carpark to check we were in the right place, but thankfully, after many minutes, we found a small group of people in running gear. They asked me how much I was running and I said that the most I had done was a 5km, so the main guy said I should go with the 2 girls. One of the girls had an injury, but seemed confident she was going to do 8km. They asked me if I wanted to do the same. I said I'd give it a try but in my head I was already planning on what to say when I got to the 5km to get me out of doing the rest. Both girls are in the teaching field and are such caring individuals. We had a wonderful conversation all the way around the route, it actually made it go so fast. Then when we got back I had to leave very soon after arriving back to the carpark. I had to get back and shower ready for when Paul arrived to take me to Santa Barbara for the scattering of dad's ashes. We chose Santa Barbara because it was a place dad really loved. From the sandy beach to the zoo with the crooked neck giraffe, from the mama and papa coffee shops to the perfect fish and chips on the end of the pier. He enjoyed just being there to tell the truth. And we wanted it to be a sea scattering because that is where dad felt the best. Whether it be on a boat out at sea or sitting on the edge of the golden sand dipping his feet into the water. Dad was a beach person. So am I really. I don't like to just sunbathe, I more enjoy the idea of sitting there watching the waves go to and fro or whilst being in that atmosphere, just sitting reading a book and taking in all the different smells you get around you.

I got into the back of Paul's car and sitting in the seat next to me was a brown plastic box. It was dad's ashes. I must admit I felt a bit weird sitting next to it, and that feeling was only going to grow when we got on the boat and have to scatter it in the sea. Would I have to use my hands? I suddenly had a pang of guilt for feeling this way about touching my dad. I started thinking about all our memories in Santa Barbara and remembered the two dolphin statue near the pier. Dad used to take about a thousand pictures of it at every angle when we would go for the day.

"Wouldn't it be great if we saw a dolphin today" I said quietly in the back of the car.

Paul didn't think we would see one because we weren't going to be going out that far. I looked out the window to the beautiful beach scenery. I so wished I could visit this beautiful place more often.

We arrived at the place and walked up to meet with everyone. We had invited both of my dads oldest friends because they were both very important to him and our family and one of them had been in our lives most of my life, and the other one all my life. Friendships that had lasted at least 33 years. That is so unique these days. Specially when they had stayed friends when we all moved to England when I was five. Long distance is such a hard thing to conquer with friendship.I walked up the stairs to the office to alert the captain we were here, but also to really ask what was actually going to happen. I have never done a sea scattering before. Infact, as far as funerals, I had only ever done burials, and none of them had been my parent, so I knew this was going to be the hardest thing to do.

He sat me down and got a box of tissues and sat them next to me. I wasn't expecting to cry right there in the captain's office just talking about the schedule, but as it happened, the captain changed from employee of the business to a son who had lost his dad not so long ago. He told me what we would do, with so much emotion as if he was talking me through the one he had done with his dad. Before I knew it I was grabbing a tissue and tears were streaming down my cheek. How was I going to face everybody now. Thank goodness I had brought sunglasses and the sun was actually out unlike England in November.

I eventually went back downstairs and then we all went over to the white and green boat. For this trip we would have a different captain. She seemed to know her stuff though. Her second in command looked like Kurt Russell's twin and he even sounded like him too. I asked captain if we might see a dolphin and she said it was unlikely as of where we were going, and the time of year, and if anyone would know, it would be the captain. I felt a little bit sad because dad would have loved that. We all got our seats and listened to the safety points. We were then off on our way.

We we plodding along and the sun was shining a perfect ray when something made me look just behind us over my left shoulder. There, almost swimming next to the boat were 2 dolphins! They were so joyful in their jumping and there's me shaking like a leaf and fumbling to get my camera out to get a picture of this brilliant present from heaven. I couldn't believe what I was seeing. I managed to get a picture of one of the fins. It was enough for me. My heart was pumping so fast because it made me feel like dad had to be close. He would not of wanted to miss this. I imagine him next to me with his camera trying just as hard to get the perfect picture of one of the dolphins. I am my father's daughter.

We get to where the special spot is, but the captain says she's going to take us to a different spot as the wind is too much here. She takes us to actually an even better place. It's opposite to the part of the beach that Paul and dad always used to stop to take pictures on the way into Santa Barbara. The captain stops the boat ready for us to start the ceremony and again I start to feel nervous. I'm very aware of how windy it is and completely worried about scattering dad's ashes and everyone just being covered in them. I've been told it will be fine if I sprinkle them out slowly and here's when I suddenly think…do I have to scoop it out with my hands? I don't know if I can do that. Dad's ashes are basically his body and bones into dust. This just makes me feel a little bit awkward to touch them. I know this sounds silly but I guess I have always been a bit funny around anything to do with death.

Matthews family is very comfortable talking about it anywhere. Everyone even has their own funeral song. They have a funeral song all picked out like flowers for a wedding. This is such a crazy thought to me, but obviously didn't put me off him as I ended up marrying into this family. I've always thought you only talk about those things till you are in retirement, not in your 30's. But then I did think my dad would live until he was actually 80 something not 68 so I guess you should be prepared anyway.

We go around everyone and ask if they would like to say something about dad and what they loved about him and then I needed to read mom's letter to dad since she was unable to come. I found this so hard because I knew this was her real feelings for him, although short, it was straight to the point and she meant every word. Tears were streaming down my face underneath my sunglasses and rolling down my cheeks. I think I used up hundreds of tissues and would still need hundred more because next I had to say my piece.

I said how much I missed him and would always love him, how he was now in a better place and I hoped he was now happy eating fish and chips somewhere here on the beach. To be honest with you, the words I said were nothing special, it was more about what was coming next after Paul said a few words. It was more about saying goodbye when I scattered the ashes that would make this trip worth the long wait. It was about giving my dad the best resting place and for him to be at peace.I was so nervous. My hands shook and not because the ship was going up and down so much but because I was nervous about letting go of my dad, because of the worry the ashes would go flying into everyone's face, because I would still miss him after doing this ceremony. I got the bag out of the brown plastic box. It was heavier than you think. Although I guess you are carrying a whole body and bones in a compact container. I started pouring the bag of grey coloured dust out into the ocean like a jug of milk onto cereal. I couldn't stop crying. The type that actually blurs your visions because of the non-stop liquid forming in your eyes.

Paul came behind me and helped hold the bag as we continued to pour it out. It was taking a long time, mainly because I did it slowly as to not get it on anyone. The thing is, I saw in the corner of my eye, my legs were covered and I had quite a bit on my hands. As soon as I noticed my hands I immediately freak out inside of me. All I wanted to do was wash it off, but we were still doing the ceremony and still scattering the ashes. Finally the bag came to an end. It was like a weight was lifted off my shoulders. Everybody had a beer to toast to dad. I couldn't. My tummy was all messed up and I could barely eat this morning in anticipation for what was to come. But I thought, perhaps tonight I would have a lovely glass of red and raise it to him.

We got back to the docks and we decided to go to the place that dad and I used to love having fish and chips from when we would have our day trips. We didn't know if it was still there but we thought we would go check. We walked to the pier and just near the gorgeous ice cream parlour and the gift shop,it stood in all its glory. It looked even better than before. Probably had a new lick of paint. I was so happy to be having food here. You couldn't get any better…however you could get cheaper. I was a little shocked at the price but thankfully Paul said he would pay for me. No doubt it's because it's right in Santa Barbara. Everything is so expensive there now.

We found a seat and got napkins and ketchup ready. Then our meal arrived. Wow! It was exactly as I remember. Beautiful fillets of fish in a crispy batter with golden chips. What a feast to be had by all. Seagulls were everywhere waiting for someone to drop even the smallest piece of food. But it didn't matter, the day had been a complete success. I couldn't wait to talk to matthew and tell him my whole experience. I knew he would be so happy for me. But it would have to wait till tomorrow morning as it was night time now in England.

As much as my body was saying it's time to go to sleep, Paul had bought tickets to go see 'Thor' at a really nice theatre and was looking forward to taking me. He had asked me if I wanted to go see the new Thor movie two weeks before I got to America, and my initial reaction was 'what is Thor?' but I could hear the enthusiasm and excitement through the phone and just went with "Do I heck! Sounds great to me".

The first thing I did after the phone call was google the film and as soon as I read the synopsis I knew this was a film I would never choose to watch in the real world. Plus this was number 3. I would have to rent (do people still do that?) the other 2 just to be on the same page as everyone else in the theatre.

Yikes. As it happens, one of my friends lent me 1 and 2 and I literally watched both the week before I left. Someone could quiz me and I would have all the answers. I felt proud.

We arrived at the theatre, got our tickets and candy (sweets) and went into cinema 1. We found our seats quickly and as I sat down I knew it would be hard to stay awake. The seats were comfy leather recliners! I mean wow! What a treat. Do people really watch a movie at a cinema like this? There was ample amount of room and all I wanted was a blanket and to fall asleep, but I turned to Paul to let him know the change of plans (I would sleep through the movie) and he just looked at me and said "Aren't these seats great, you are going to love watching this movie like this" I think in my 'half asleep' state I raised a thumb at him. This was going to be a task.

Thank goodness this movie was the funniest out of the 3, because it came to the end and I actually was still awake. Awake, but my eyes drifting every few minutes and me jumping when my head slipped down. We left and walked towards the car only stopping for a burger on the way to eat in the car. Probably the messiest burger I have ever had but definitely delicious. A bit of an empty place for such tasty food, but I guess their customers must come either earlier or later. I would definitely go back at another day and experience having a sit down meal here. I looked at the time on my phone. I had got into the habit of eating so late, and worse than that, I was hungry all the time. It was going to be hard to go back home and eat smaller portions and more healthy ingredients, but I would be doing that because I want to get my life back in order, and losing weight would do just that. I got back to Susan's and she was waiting up for me. We had our pre bedtime chat (shorter than usual) and then I went to bed into a deep sleep till at least 3:30am.

# Chapter 21: Sunday…

I slept in till 3:30am this morning which was good for me, but I still felt like I needed a days sleep to catch up. I was partially excited and partially nervous, as this morning I was doing a talk at Josh's church about decluttering. I wanted to inspire people and change peoples lives so that they appreciate everything that is great in their lives. At the same time I have great stage fright. The lucky thing was that I had just done this talk at my church's 'ladies night', so I was very familiar with the contents and should hopefully flow quite well.

I have a deep red dress that Matthew bought me as a Christmas gift one year. I had borrowed it from my sister-in-law once (in a much smaller size which meant I had to cover the zip not going fully up with a cardigan). Whenever I wear it I feel particularly confident and pretty. I don't think

being pretty is important to do a talk but I do think that if a woman thinks she is pretty than her confidence flies high.
For this reason, I wore it for the talk. I also wore my favourite heels as I stand much taller with them (at only 5'1 this isn't hard).
Susan and Dan said they would both come to listen to the talk and then we could go to the Getty museum afterwards. I was excited to see Josh and his wife Rachel and their beautiful little girl Sammy. Also his mum and dad would be there and I looked forward to catching up with them properly since the last time I saw them it had to be a quick visit. When we arrived Josh's dad Tillman was outside sweeping and everyone else was inside making the church look beautiful.
We walked in and I introduced everyone to each other and then I set up the pictures and videos that were going to go with my talk with Josh. Then before I knew it, the time had come when we all sat down for Pastor Josh and he would introduce me. April came with her beautiful family and I met a few sweet members of the community, but this was a small church in comparison to all the ones I had been to. This had to be because nobody knew that it was a church and a great one at that, because it was in a school hall. With the proper amount of advertisement people would flock there because Josh definitely has a big passion and a fire burning inside him. He will go far in life I think.I finished my talk and felt pleased with how it went. I wished it hadn't finished. I wanted to do more.
What a great way to inspire people. I had pictures taken with all my beautiful second family for a wonderful memory for years to come, and then we got in our car and left to go to the famous Getty museum full of amazing artwork!
The moment we arrived I remembered how gorgeous the surrounding

were. I couldn't wait to see the gardens. Those metal trees that bloomed with different shades of pink floral at the top. The tunnels of foliage around the base of the garden and the waterfall that calmed your very being by just watching it. We decided to have a look at the art work and then follow it by the gardens to end on a high note. By golly there is a lot of artwork in this place. I think really you need two full days to be able to see it all with enough time to do it in a relaxed manner. We had just a couple of hours, but if all I got to see was a small amount of art and all of the gardens I would be thrilled. It had been a long time since I was last here, and it was with dad. The memories flooded in. We both really enjoyed going and always found ourselves much more inspired to do something amazing after a visit. We had a lovely lunch in the restaurant their. Susan and I had some beef sandwiches and Dan had a peanut butter and jelly(jam) sandwich. They had all sorts of food to eat but the beef in my sandwich was amazing. Nowhere in England would you get a rare roast beef sandwich and yet this is how beef is meant to be eaten. We collected all our things and got back into the car to go home and get ready for the evening at the factory of cheesecake with my friends I used to teach with. This was going to be fun because I loved these girls so much and because I really missed them. I also loved the food there…well the dinners are great…but the cheesecake was amazing, and I had my eye on a special one that I had only heard about recently. The pecan-pumpkin cheesecake. It did not disappoint and I only wish they had this place in my town in England. Although that would mean I would be there all the time and that would get expensive over time. It's always nice to meet up with old friends specially when it's a bunch of girls and you can just laugh together. I can't tell you how much I needed that right now. It turned out to be so much fun and I didn't want it to stop and then remember I was fatherless again. That's the thing about fun times. They have to finish at some point and when we stop, that's when we start to think about current situations, and for me, that was remembering dad had died and I missed him. We got back home and had our usual before bedtime chat over a glass of red wine, and before long I couldn't keep my eyes open so bedtime it was for me.

# Chapter 22: Monday…

This morning I get to spend most of the morning with my dear friend Lily and her sweet child (well…she's now a teenager I guess) Julie. I love her so much. She just completely speaks her mind and is not afraid to say what she believes in. Basically if you are secretly thinking it…Lily is saying it. What you see is what you get and that's what I love the most. There's no guessing game of whether she likes me or not, you will know if she likes you or not. She's always got a massive smile and that truly makes you cheery for the rest of the day. But don't let that confuse you that she's one of those chirpy cheep cheep morning people…she needs her coffee just as much as me.

She's also got a fun accent. To me she sounds like she's from New York a lot of the time with a tiny Cuban twang on a couple of words. I like to imagine her asking for a cup of Joe whilst wrapped up in a Cuban flag…But doesn't everyone?…nope just me? Ok let's move on! She will always be my friend because we both have a mutual respect for each other and that is really something to hold onto. If you find that in a friendship, hold on to it like a 2 year old and their favourite teddy.

Julie is very sweet and kind like her mum and has a very big smile from ear to ear. She wears braces but just like 'Mary' from the movie 'Something about Mary', they almost make her more beautiful than she already is. I guess just some people make metal in the mouth look great, I know it was the complete opposite for me. Julie has a thick American accent but she is much much quieter than most American teenagers. She has an amazing talent when it comes to all things creative and thankfully for me, she shares it on social media.

She has a twinkle in her eye looking for travel opportunities and to learn new things, but to me she will always be 5, walking around bookshops with me and her mum.

We meet up at our favourite book shop that has a café in it with the best coffee in it. When she arrives I notice she looks different. She's gained more weight and now is walking with a cane. What the heck happened since October? My honest feeling was "would I see her again before she leaves this world?" what a scary thought to think of. I couldn't handle losing another loved one so soon after dad, and I guess since losing him, it has opened my eyes up to how healthy people are and it kind of scares me a little but I want to make sure I don't lose anybody else who is precious to me.I was so worried for her health. I, unlike Lily, find it hard to bring up difficult things to people. So I thought I would talk to her about life and then see where she was and then maybe bring it up casually.

We had a lovely catch up and she talked to me about having to move away from Santa Clarita because the heat was affecting her MS, and how she was private tutoring now instead of teaching, but was enjoying it. I still thought it was not a good time to bring up how I felt so I thought I might email her later about it. I'm so much better at writing my feelings down than having to fumble through words in front of someone. Once I was back home I did email her and she had been struggling with health issues, but has starting losing weight and has proven to be really successful with one of the weight loss plans. She's doing well so I feel happier now.

As our time was coming to an end we went to the far end of the book shop, to my favourite part…the journals. There were so many I wanted but decided to sleep on it and if I really couldn't do without it, I would get it in the morning.

We said our goodbyes and then I walked up the road to a yummy Mexican restaurant to meet up with my favourite teacher of all time. Wendy Ruiz. She taught me everything I ever needed to know about childcare, but not only that but also how to be a decent human being. She has the most beautiful heart and I feel so privileged that not only she taught me, but she became my friend too. She's similar in height to me (short) and her smile is from ear to ear. She has this gorgeous big fluffy hair and she has an amazing amount of energy.

When she gets here we decide to eat outside because the weather is too beautiful to be staying indoors, and she is right, back in England it's been raining.

We catch up on life and how she is and her family and it's actually a really relaxing time. It felt good talking to someone and not worry about what the kids were doing. Not worrying about hot food and drinks being spilt or pushed over. We have a big hug not knowing when we will see each other again and just like that, she had to leave. Tonight I am cooking dinner for Susan and Dan, it's the best way I know to say thank you for letting me stay. With a delicious homemade lasagne! Everyone loves food and everyone I know loves a good lasagne! I got the ingredients and then with every ounce of love I had in me that day, I specially crafted the best dinner I could possibly do. I wanted them to really enjoy it and relax and take in the night.

They deserved it since they had been so kind to me and really looked after me.When it came out of the oven I felt really pleased with my masterpiece although ever so slightly different to my usual, but I had to work with all new American ingredients that I wasn't used to. I plate it up with salad and garlic bread and gave the plates out. Well, if actions are anything to go by, they both had seconds, so hopefully that meant I did a great job.

We had an in depth chat that was followed by pudding/candy! Dan loves his candy bars (chocolate bars) and before long more than a few had been eaten. It came to 7:30pm and my next meeting was upon us. I was getting picked up by a sweet family that I taught both children when they were 5. Well this was no 5 year old that came to the door to escort me to the car. By golly he was a man! How had he grown so much? He was taller than me, which I know is not difficult, but he was a giant. How time had flown by since the last time I saw him 8 years ago.

This family have been in my life since their eldest, had started in my class. I used to babysit him and his brother, and once in a while I would go on day trips with them. I love them so much. I wish I could bring them

over to England to live over here. When I moved here, my dad used to go visit them every Christmas for a catch up and to tell them about me and my kids and the boys really enjoyed all of my dads stories.
Then March 2017 I got an email from their mum Karen when I had just got into bed, asking if my dad was ok because he didn't come to see them this past Christmas and they hadn't heard from him in ages. The thing is they really only saw him at Christmas, it was their special time for catching up, so they didn't even know he had cancer since he was diagnosed in April '16 and passed away January '17. I felt awful again. Not only would I have to explain that he had cancer but that he had died too.
I asked Karen to call me. It was going to be easier than sending a long message, and probably a lot more personal. My phone rang not too long after that and as I picked it up my heart raced. I was nervous to tell her because I knew they all adored my dad. It was heartbreaking. When she answered the phone you could tell she wasn't expecting anything near to what I was about to tell her and this made me sad. When I broke the news to her, it was the most amount of sadness I had heard in a person's voice since the memorial service. She truly missed him and didn't really know how to reply apart from saying sorry to me for my loss. I wanted to hug her, but with being in a different country than her it made it even more hard.
We hung up and then I lay back down to bed. Not to sleep, but to just take in the feelings I had running around my head and try and breathe again. Anyway, back to now, and we got back to their house, the same one I used to babysit in. We talked over a beautiful mug of red velvet chocolate rooibos tea, in one of my favourite glass mugs they have. If you

have never tried this flavoured tea you must. It actually is very subtle as far as the chocolatey taste but very satisfying. It was so lovely to hear what the boys were up to and what they love to do now. I quickly got a picture with them all before I headed back to Susan's house for bed and to rest of for the next days festivities. I really hoped I would see them again soon, and hopefully the next time wouldn't be as big of a change in all of them.

# Chapter 23: Tuesday…

Up again early this morning and then we did something I haven't done for a while but really enjoy…we sat in our pj's and chatted for ages, relaxed and not in a rush. As a mum of two young children, it is very hard to get time like this for yourself, but it is a must to have once in a while. So that morning we got through two coffees quite quickly and I was absolutely sure they wouldn't be my last ones for the day.

I had mentioned to Susan that one thing I really wanted back in October was some specialty French toast bites that this one drive through used to make when I lived there. Back in October I ask Paul if we could go there and he conned me in believing that they didn't do them anymore…well, I got myself some research and it turns out…he was completely lying to my face! So Susan and I got dressed, we got our bags and headed to the closest one to us.

I walked in and there was only one thing I wanted. I ordered it as quickly as I could, found a seat and sat there eagerly waiting for that highly greased fried toast to make its way to me. When it came to the table it looked just as good as it did 8 years ago. In fact the powdered sugar on top actually glistened. It was beautiful and tasted like all my dreams had come true. Unfortunately they only lasted 5 minutes and then every crumb was gone. We got our bags and went back home. I decided with the little time I had before meeting up with friends, I would do a 5km run to help get rid of some of the thousands of calories I had eaten this week. I ran all along the roads close by and up on a hill able to see a wonderful view of Santa Clarita with all the blue sky above.

Why is it when I lived here I didn't appreciate how beautiful this place is? Why did I never go for a run here? I wish I had taken time out and taken one run as a teen, I'm sure I would have got into it and might just have been the one exercise to stop me getting to the size I did before I left. I got back and felt good to have done that whilst still away.

My next meeting was at lunch at a famous Italian chain. It was to meet my friends Noelle and Barb again. Boy I love seeing them. They always make me smile, and they are both such wonderful people. They both actually make the world a better place. I'm not just saying that, Barb actually has been arranging blood drives for the hospital that her kids go to every other week, and Noelle home schools her kids, that's how much she want to make a difference to her kids education!

We all love this Italian restaurant. Most people love it because of the breadsticks, I actually love the salad, which is weird because I don't ever believe you should go to a restaurant and order a salad…apart from this place. And when you do, make sure you ask for it with ranch dressing. It works better and the best bit…it's unlimited! My other favourite is their alfredo pasta. Best pasta sauce ever. It's thick and rich and cheesy and it also works very well as a dipping sauce for those amazing breadsticks. Heck, if you gave me just a spoon I would be happy. But this time I didn't have the pasta because they had a lunch deal, and I'm all for a yummy meal cheaper. So I had a kind of Italian quesadilla. A tortilla filled with tomatoes, peppers, herbs and cheese. Very yummy and just the right size for a lunch meal. We caught up on each others lives and had fun just chatting to each other face to face. And before long, our meal was finished and  it was time for them to go.

They offered me a lift, but I thought this would be a perfect time to add some more exercise into this time away, so I said I would walk. This was funny because I had to cross a massive road and in America a lot of the red lights have a certain amount of time to cross the road. My heart felt like it was pumping so hard, people could see it through my top. I honestly felt so anxious just to cross this road. And self conscious about the way I was rushing my tiny feet and legs across this huge road. I got across the road with 1 second remaining thank goodness, but my heart was beating fast and I was just praying there were no more of those roads to cross for the rest of the journey.

The funny thing is, in England this is the one thing I complain about. The roads in England always seem too small for me and I'm always so glad I don't drive just yet, because some of the roads, where there are cars parked on both sides and you have to drive down it, those roads completely scare me. I always hold my breath when Matthew has to drive down one. As I do with all my shocking experiences, I went straight to social media. Susan must have read my post because she was on the phone 2 minutes later offering to pick me up! I was actually relieved. I got to go back 'home' and enjoy some more beautiful catch up time. Before long it was time to leave to go meet up with my friend Leah at the local coffee shop (you know the type…one on every corner…literally).

I only had an hour before Paul was going to pick me up to take me out to dinner. I was just glad to have any time with her. She is such a beautiful person and when I'm with her she always makes me smile. While waiting for her to arrive, I looked around at the endless coffee memorabilia. I just love mugs and if I had gone with lots more money I would have been coming home with lots more mugs. Matthew is probably quite pleased we don't have lots of money at this point because our house does not need anymore at all. I love the big tall mugs that hold 2 mugfuls of coffee and they always make your hands look small. You don't get many mugs like that in England.

Anyway, Leah arrived and we had a catch up about how her beautiful daughters were doing and how her eldest had chosen her college. I talked about how smart my kids are and how much I miss them. Then my phone rang. It was Paul. He was outside ready to meet me. Time had gone so fast but was happy for the small amount we got together. And now for dinner. Paul was taking me to that wonderful burger place again. I couldn't believe my luck. My tummy rumbled just thinking about my first bite.

As we walked in, I mentally made a note of the exact burger I wanted so I could quickly jot it down on the order form and then it wouldn't take too much longer to get to me. Paul told me to add pork to the top (on top of the bacon and the burger patty that had bacon in it too) I reassured him that what I was ordering was exactly what I wanted. He took the form and as the waiter came up and took them, he quickly ticked the box that said 'added pork' on mine. I knew I would come close to being sick, but there was nothing I could do about it. He asked me if I wanted any sides, which shocked me a little as I really didn't have the room for all this extra food. But he said "I'm sure you will share these with me". I know I would have a mouthful, just out of being polite, but I also knew that would be it. He decided to order wings, chips and onion rings. Someone was going to bring food home with them. I remember the size of the plates in there and the height of the pile of chips. Starving people should only attempt this, or people who haven't eaten for days and days.We had our burgers and as predicted after one wing, two chips and one onion ring I was ready to pop. Paul on the other hand must have an empty, boot because he was just wafting it down with ease. We packed up whatever was left and walked back to the car.

# Chapter 24: Wednesday…

This morning I woke up excited for the day. Paul had half the day off and was going to spend it with me. It reminded me of when we were younger and we would go to the cinema together. I used to love it. We haven't always been close, but when we have the rare moments where we spend time together, I actually really treasure it. But what would we be doing today? It was a bit of a secret. He wanted to surprise me. My heart smiled at that thought. We were headed to the city of Los Angeles, the city of angels, where I got my name from. Paul, months ago, booked tickets to go to this famous art museum and it was going to be a real treat for me. Something I really loved to do was take time to look at art, even if I don't quite understand it, just trying to is a fun activity to do once in a while. I love the drive up there too. It's exciting. Tall buildings. Exotic restaurants.

Glamorous shops. My camera took a beating and I can only imagine how many photos I had taken on this trip. When i'm on holiday, I most enjoy the artistic side of pictures and always find amazing scenes that could easily have 30 different shots of brilliance, depending on how you are standing.

When we got there, Paul took me to a sweet little restaurant where they make katsu curry with many degrees of spice. Paul said I could definitely handle a 5 or 6 (with 10 being the spiciest) I asked the waiter what he had there and he said he's never gone above a 4. So I decided I would give a 4 a go. Well, i'm not sure what kind of people actually attempt a 10 (although i'm pretty sure Chris had an 8 or 9) but the 4 was pretty hot. Probably a little too hot for my liking, but still very tasty. I chose chicken, but like usual Paul had the pork. It was delicious. Very filling though and they really pile it on your plate. We left very satisfied and excited for what we were about to see.

We finally arrived at this very modern white building. Tall and clean. Nothing too special on the outside, but that so far on my trips has meant nothing. There are lots of windows at the bottom of this building and in one small corner there's the shop and to the other side there are stairs leading to the 'special' art gallery and to the far right, where we are going, is the main gallery. Everything looks very new and there are lots of pieces of art with bright colours, some neon. We got through to one room that has a massive table and chairs. This was by far my favourite piece. I took the token picture of Paul and myself underneath the table standing. We had a really wonderful time and I will always treasure those memories I can take back with me. We walked out and behind the gallery is a restaurant that has a fire pit with outside seating. We instantly gravitated to this. We decided to stay there for nibbles and a glass of wine. If ever there was a time that I felt very grown up it was there. Or should I say sophisticated. Matching the conversation with the beautifully chilled white wine and the crispy potatoes, dunking them in the aioli listening to the trees sway to the light breeze. I could do with that every night.

When we had finished we got back into the car and without me knowing my brother drove me to a special donut shop that give you fresh hot donuts out of the grease. I wanted to go last time but I just ran out of time, so this made my day. I even got a donut hat. We walked in and there was a long line, but I heard someone say to me

"Would you like a sample?"

Well, there was no way I was going to say no. I knew I would still be getting one, but a sample couldn't hurt on the way up to the counter. I look up to take it from the girl who offered it to me, and to my amazement it was a whole donut! A sample in this shop is an actual full blown donut. I grinned from ear to ear and accepted it with both hands. It was delicious and hot but I was almost positive I couldn't eat another. I'm not sure how many Paul bought but I'm completely sure it was more than one! That boy can eat a lot of donuts! We got back in the car and drove home with full bellies.

# Chapter 25: Thursday…

Well this is my last day in the US. Always a sad time for me, but also happy to be seeing my family again. I arranged to see some of my friends this morning. I have tried to see them all in either the October trip or the January trip but they could not make it. So i'm sitting in the coffee shop waiting for the first friend and shes a bit late so I message her to just check i'm at the right coffee place and she replies with that she completely forgot and now can't make it. Another said she was busy could we meet up another time even after in this same week i mentioned when my last day was. I'm not being funny but, i don't come to America all the time and the last time i saw these people was 10 years ago. If the tables had turned i would not have missed any meeting. I just would have made the effort to even go even if it was just for 5 minutes. I didn't feel angry or that i would just drop a friendship because of this, however i still felt sad, but life will go on. The other friend turned up, late but she did warn me, and it was actually amazing to get to chat with her again. We are both mummies now which we weren't the last time we saw each other. We discussed each others lives and how we had both changed. We finished our drinks and conversation and then said our goodbyes. I hoped it wouldn't be long before I saw her again.

Susan picked me up and we headed back to her place to do a bit more packing and to get ready to see my friend Nancy one last time before I go. We are going to meet at my favourite taco place and hopefully meet my brother on his lunch break as one last goodbye as Susan is taking me to the airport today. I have fit every last thing I can possibly take with me back home to remind me of dad, and there are still things here I can't take. One day I'll be back for them but for now they will have to stay here. My bag is the heaviest it has ever been, but still within regulations thank goodness. As much as I have really felt the benefit of this trip and having a real goodbye to my dad, it has taken a lot out of me. I do feel like when I get home I can start to properly move on. Not forget or never have a sad day again, but possibly learn to find ways of liking life again.

Susan takes me to the shops for one last trip for things to bring home, to get the things I will really miss. Things like ranch dressing powder, biscuit mixes, and yummy scoops crisps. That will probably last me a couple of days when I get back and then I can go back to healthy eating. We then get back in the car and drive to meet Nancy. This weather has been so beautiful whilst I have been here. Cooler in the mornings but nothing too bad. You would need to wear a jumper but by 9 or 10 the latest it's off and

warm…in November! I do wish I could swap weather sometimes. I'm not looking forward to going back to the British cold wet weather.
We arrive and I suddenly can't decide what to have, obviously it's going to be tacos, but which ones? One of each flavour I think. I think when I get home my mission will be to find a decent Mexican restaurant close to my town. We order and go sit down at the table Paul is sitting with his friend waiting around for us. I know that this is the last meal we will have together for probably years now, and it makes me feel a little sad inside. To think years ago when we were young I took meals together for granted and thought it wasn't anything special. Paul only has a short lunch break so he finishes up and then hugs me goodbye like he would see me there again tomorrow. I know he has done this because he hates goodbyes. I feel so sad to be saying goodbye to him, and I know I keep saying this, but I really don't think i'll be seeing him again any time soon. There are no more reasons to go over and no more extra cash I can splurge on another trip over. This is definitely it till i'm rich and famous, or till he can afford to come over to see me. I try to hold the emotions in but it's so hard. I keep watching till he has driven away. I start up a conversation about the yummy churros to make me not feel sad anymore and it works.
Eventually it's time to say goodbye to Nancy and get into the car and head out to the airport. There's something about heading to the airport that unsettles me. I always have a funny feeling in my tummy because I always know when I get to the airport and i've gone through security, that's when I know there's no going back, i'm going home and that goodbye I just did at the stairs to Susan was the last time i'll see her for a while. It's like a dull sadness in the pit of your belly that you can't shake. It fades the closer you get to home and are greeted by your loving family

who give you cuddles like they haven't seen you in a month, but it doesn't properly ever go away.

The moment I woke up the next day, I was sad. It was a different kind of sad from when I came back from the January trip, but still sad. But what I had learnt from this was that one day you can feel like this and then the next day perhaps 4 or 5 or even 2 weeks you'll be fine. It comes in waves someone told me and they were right.

# Chapter 26: One year on…

January came around very quickly and I really didn't want to face it. There were a few things I could do to avoid it. Bury myself in massive piles of all my favourite foods for the rest of the month, go back to bed everyday after dropping the kids to school or I could embrace it with all the fire built up in me to make my dad proud of me. I had seen a lot of people on one of my running groups speaking about something called 'Red January'. It stands for Run Every Day January. Yes that does sound very intense, specially when you have two little kids who still keep you up in the night, but January is a hard month for me, so with every ounce of willpower, I committed to this challenge.

Some mornings I would literally just do the 1.6km from school drop off to home, but that was still an accomplishment and it made me feel positive about the next day ahead. About half way through I was struggling, but what kept me going was just thinking to myself, this will make dad proud up there wherever he is, hopefully in heaven, smiling down at me. If that wasn't enough, I also challenged myself to do fifty miles in the month of January. In comparison, most months I do about half of the required miles, so I would be doubling it and that was challenge enough. I ended my last day, the one year anniversary of dad passing, getting to 60 miles, stopping half way at the beach to pay my respects to my hero, and then heading back to have a mug of hot black coffee from my dad's mug. Later I would have fish and chips for dinner as that was one of dad's favourite meals, and somehow made me feel like he was around me when I had it. I think it's important to mark these days. Cry if you feel you need to. Smile at the beautiful memories, do what you think is best, but then go back to life the next day. This has got me to where I am today, among other things, and I truly believe it's the best thing to do with grief.

Today is another day, I wake up and I do still feel sad but I get up and get out the door, and try to get on with the day ahead instead of mopping around extending the sad feelings from the day before.

So I'm sat in another yummy coffee house, sipping my beautifully crafted frothy coffee. I've had time to put my contacts in with ease and apply just enough make-up to feel pretty. I'm sitting in a seat that has just the right amount of natural light, and it's quiet enough to hear myself think, but noisy enough to create a small amount of atmosphere. I should feel on top of the world.

I don't.

There's a sad feeling in my gut that's bubbling up inside of me. I can feel it tighten in my throat. I miss dad. This happens from time to time. It's not new and without a doubt in my mind it will happen again. People say, your sadness for your loss won't ever go away, it will just get easier to live with. I can't see this ever getting easier. Sure it's not everyday now after a year, so in that way it is easier, and i no longer have that heavy black cloud over me, but when I have a bad day, it hits me hard from the moment I wake up.

I still think i'm in shock. How long does that last? I know when I scattered my dad's ashes it helped, but it still hasn't made me get over the shock. I still see a picture of him and in complete disarray in my head, I still think and feel deep in my heart, "I can't believe he's gone" "I can't believe cancer killed him". It still feels like it happened just the other day. I get up everyday now and try my hardest to find the great things in my life and focus on them. That's the only way to start to live again. To work through life with this added emotion, floating around your body. I know dad would want me to be getting on and enjoying all the beauty the world has to offer. He would not want me to be letting it all go over my head and blend into the distance.

He would have been so proud to have seen how far I have come. In 3 weeks I will be doing a 10k run. I'm entering writing competitions. Ok...not winning them, but i'm putting myself out there. I've also written this book that will hopefully be published. And although I have gone through a magnitude of crap, I am brave to get through losing my dad, especially from the way he was taken and how traumatic it was for me. I am a new and different person as I have changed because of having to lose my hero but...Take me as I am, because this is how i'm going to be, and that's ok.

I'm going to go through life appreciating every moment, and not take anything for granted now. I'm going to do new experiences. I'm going to work hard on getting my dreams and only look back at the good memories. I will make videos of the people who mean the world to me. I will be that mum that carries a camera with her at all times to ensure not to miss any special moments. And life will be lived.

I will not become that slug, black as night, that I passed some time ago in the street. I may have been in my cocoon but I now must fly like the butterfly my heart desires to be.

As I walked to go pick up the kids from school, in a haze full of my new promises to myself, a bright blue pearlescent butterfly fluttered around me, as if to remind me of the promises I just made.

And just like that, it flew off as if in its victory.

To be continued...

Steve Tuffill
30/03/1948- 31/01/2017

# Thank you!

Thank you to my husband, Matthew Mackrell, for always being there for me and encouraging me to do what I love. Thank you for helping me through this very hard time in my life and being my rock throughout. I love you with all my heart x

For Marlia and Milo, without you two I would have found it even harder to get through the hard times. I love you both so very much x

Thank you to my mum, Carol Tuffill, for always helping me have some quality quiet time to do my writing and for babysitting whenever you can. I couldn't have finished without your help. Lots of love x

Thank you Paul Tuffill for the amazing encouragement to do this book and for getting me through the hard times. You are my favourite brother x

For all my extended family and family I have adopted x

For my church Elim Worthing. My constant house of love and my home group for giving me an overwhelming amount of support x

To Sam Stoner for the amazing artwork on the front cover. IT's everything I wanted it to be and more x

Thank you to Virgin Atlantic airlines for helping me when I needed to change my tickets x

Thank you to all my friends, old and new, who have supported me throughout the years with encouragement and reading lots of snippets of creative writing pieces x

Thank you to Writer's HQ for a brilliant Writers Retreat in Worthing x

Thank you to Ermias Yosef for being my human computer. You have helped me so much and I really appreciate it x

Thank you Emily Brown (A Dimensions Series books) for being all the answered questions to publishing a book x

Thank you to my wonderful editor Amanda Williams with Dark Raven Edits for editing the book and giving me great advice x

Thank you to Naomi Meyer Newland and Uflourish for literally changing my life x

Thank you Marriotts preschool in Goring and Mrs Brock, Mrs Stafford, Mrs Phillips, Mrs Borgars, Mrs Laurence, Mrs DeLuca and Abbie for providing important excellent education for both my kids whilst I have written this, and for being a tower of support that I feel so lucky to have had x

35712312R00094

Printed in Poland
by Amazon Fulfillment
Poland Sp. z o.o., Wrocław

Thank you Goring Primary school and Mrs Jee, Miss Leach and Mrs Taylor, for providing amazing 'big' school education for my daughter 5 days a week whilst I write this book x

Thank you Senseo coffee pods and Starbucks coffee for keeping me caffeinated!

Thank you to America for the following things: Great food, beaches, weather, zoo's, coffee houses, and book shops.

And thank you to all my readers. I hope you have enjoyed reading my book and are looking forward to my next one x

American Teabag 2 and 3 will be out later in 2019. Visit my webpage and let me know what you think of the book at:

https://atuffill.wixsite.com/angiemackrell-author